THE
EARLY HISTORY
OF
TOLLAND

THE EARLY HISTORY OF TOLLAND

An Address, Delivered Before the Tolland County Historical Society, at Tolland, Connecticut, on the 22ND Day of August and 27TH Day of September, 1861

BY

Loren P. Waldo

President of Said Society

HERITAGE BOOKS
2013

HERITAGE BOOKS
AN IMPRINT OF HERITAGE BOOKS, INC.

Books, CDs, and more—Worldwide

For our listing of thousands of titles see our website
at
www.HeritageBooks.com

A Facsimile Reprint
Published 2013 by
HERITAGE BOOKS, INC.
Publishing Division
100 Railroad Ave. #104
Westminster, Maryland 21157

Copyright © 1986 Heritage Books, Inc.

Originally published
Hartford:
Press of Case, Lockwood & Company
1861

— Publisher's Notice —
In reprints such as this, it is often not possible to remove blemishes from the original. We feel the contents of this book warrant its reissue despite these blemishes and hope you will agree and read it with pleasure.

International Standard Book Numbers
Paperbound: 978-1-55613-004-5
Clothbound: 978-0-7884-6974-9

NOTICE.

When I first commenced the preparation of the following pages, I only expected to write an address that might have occupied an hour in its reading before the Historical Society for whom I was preparing it; but I soon found the subject too extensive and interesting to be thus summarily disposed of. I accordingly enlarged my original plan somewhat, and although my time was too limited to exhaust the several topics touched upon, yet I can not but believe that enough has been done to render the numerous facts I have recorded worthy of preservation, so that they may become available to him who shall undertake to complete what I have but imperfectly begun. Most of the address was read before the Tolland County Historical Society, at two meetings convened for that purpose, and such was the interest manifested in the subject that very many expressed a strong desire to see the address in print. A proposition was made to have it published in numbers in the Tolland County Record, and I assented to an arrangement by which I supposed this would be carried into effect. I therefore set about revising the address and preparing it for publication, in doing which I availed myself of the kindness and assistance of my friend, Sidney Stanley, Esq., who has carefully compared the principal facts with records and his own memoranda, collected by the labor of years. And I would, in this place, acknowledge my obligations to him for his valuable aid in collecting and collating very much of the material contained in these pages.

Having finished the revision of the address, and the paper in whose columns it was designed to appear having suspended, I have by the

NOTICE.

advice of some of my friends, ventured to print it in a pamphlet form, at my own expense, trusting that some of the sons of Tolland whose history I have endeavored to perpetuate, will be willing to contribute something towards the expenses of publication, by buying copies for their own use. To them I cheerfully submit the work, and whatever of merit or demerit it may contain, I have some hope it will, at least, be the means of rescuing some incidents from oblivion that might otherwise have been forever lost; and if it shall awaken any interest in the subject of local history, I shall be fully compensated for the labor I have expended.

Dated at Tolland, this 10th day of December, 1861.

LOREN P. WALDO.

ADDRESS.

GENTLEMEN OF THE TOLLAND COUNTY HISTORICAL SOCIETY,
AND FELLOW CITIZENS:

MY present purpose is to speak of the early history of the town of Tolland, and to gather up and preserve some mementos of the persons who first peopled its territory. The feeling that prompts to this duty is a sacred one and should be cherished; for while we are ruminating among the tombs of our ancestors and gathering relics of departed worth, we can not fail to be deeply impressed with the thought that the footsteps of time are fast effacing the most prominent transactions and will soon obliterate the last trace of all things earthly. We should most instinctively love to cultivate the remembrance of past events; to let our affections cluster around the memories of those departed ones whose stations we occupy; and to look forward with fervent hope to that period in our own existence when kindred spirits will commingle in one promiscuous throng. In these exercises we may learn wisdom from the experience of the illustrious dead; may profit by their spotless examples; may be encouraged to imitate their never-dying virtues;—and to follow more cheerfully in their shining track through life's stormy mazes to the haven of immortal happiness and peace.

In looking back through the long vista of years since this town was first known, we can discover no incident of thrilling interest connected with its history. We can point to no spot where the white and the red man have met in mortal combat; nor where hostile armies have sought for vengeance in the bloody encounter. We do not know that the barbarian war-fire has ever shone upon these hills; or that the savage war-whoop was ever heard in these valleys. We have no legend of the Indian's stealthy tread—of his merciless attack upon the innocent and defenceless; or of our soil ever reeking with human blood. Nor can we find the footsteps of any distinguished personage upon its territory who has attracted the gaze of the world by his deeds of daring or acts of self-devotion. The history of Tolland, in short, is not calculated to interest the marvelous, nor produce wonder and astonishment in the reflecting; but like a gentle current, bears upon its quiet bosom facts worthy of our notice, and which may afford us both instruction and amusement.

The territory now called Tolland, prior to the year 1700, formed a part of the vast wilderness that covered the western continent before the track of civilization ever visited these shores, and was inhabited only by wild beasts or wilder men. The town of Mansfield was settled about this period, and as the inhabitants of that town had some connection with the people of Windsor it is probable that in their intercourse the hills of Tolland first attracted their notice. This town was originally a part of the township of Windsor, and the earliest records to be found in the town are copies of the transactions of the town of Windsor in relation to the lands included in the town of Tolland. The earliest of these records I have been able to find is under date of April 18th, 1713, at which time a committee was appointed " to lay out a settlement upon the east side of Windsor upon lands formerly purchased of the Indians." This committee performed the duties assigned them and made a report of their doings commencing in these words:

"A chronicle of the acts of the committee empowered by the town of Windsor to lay out a plantation from the east side of Windsor upon lands formerly purchased of the Indians, April 18, 1713. The committee went upon the land to be laid out, and laid out and bounded highways and several lots as followeth. A highway of twenty rods in breadth, and running due north upon the hill called *the meeting-house hill*, between the first furlong of lots on the said hill on the east side of the highway and the second furlong of lots on west side of the highway; and is marked out by several marked trees, and stakes and heaps of stones, and goes the same breadth and point of compass until it pass the brook that runs up out of Cedar Swamp."

Then follows a record of seventeen lots of land containing forty acres each, laid out on each side of this highway,—eight of them being on the east side of the highway, bounding west upon it, and nine lots being on the west side of the same, bounding east upon it. These lots were each forty rods in width and one hundred and sixty rods in length, being forty rods upon the highway and extending one hundred and sixty rods in rear from the same. One of the lots on the east side of the highway is bounded north on the brook, which is no doubt the stream that runs up out of Cedar Swamp. The lots on the east side were numbered from one to eight inclusive, and were granted by the committee to Samuel Pinney, Jr., Hezekiah Porter, Sergt. Henry Wolcott, Joseph Porter, Nathan Gillett, and Samuel Forward. Those on the west side were numbered from one to nine inclusive, and were granted to Enoch Loomis, Cornelius Birge, Simon Wolcott, Jr., Joshua Loomis, Sergt. Henry Wolcott, Noah Grant, Joseph Rockwell, Jr., Thomas Grant, and Josiah Rockwell. The first and sixth lots on the east side of the highway do not appear to have been assigned to any one.

It has been a matter of some inquiry where this first highway was located, for it is evident that its location was intended to establish the center of the new town. From the record we learn that it was "twenty rods in breadth," and ran "due north upon the hill called meeting-house hill, between the first furlong of lots on the said hill on the east side of the highway, and the second furlong of lots on the west side of the highway," and that it goes the same breadth and point of "compass until it pass the brook that runs up out of Cedar Swamp." Here we have the point of compass—"due north,"—the width of the road—"twenty rods,"—the name of the hill where located—"meeting-house hill,"—and its northern terminus—"the brook that runs up out of Cedar Swamp." Now is there any locality that will answer this description?

Some persons have supposed that the village of Tolland is located on this highway. The street, they say, runs nearly north and south, sufficiently to answer the description "*due north;*" that it is, or was before trespassed upon and shorn of its primeval capaciousness, nearly of the requisite width; that it is the only eminence in town that can be justly called meeting-house hill, for no other hill was ever honored with an edifice of this character, and the stream of water north of the village, known as "Spencer brook," is the brook that was described as running up out of Cedar Swamp. But a little attention will satisfy the casual observer that the present village could not have been the locality described in this record. For the course of the street is not "*due north*," but several degrees to the west of north, and before we come to Spencer brook it is north-east. Nor was the street ever twenty rods wide, during its whole length, nor is there any evidence that it was ever called "meeting-house hill." It must be borne in mind that this record was made April 18, 1713, more than two years before the charter of the town was granted, and before its locality or extent could be known. The town of Coventry was incorporated in 1711, but its northern boundary was not then established, as we shall hereafter have occasion to see; and hence the proper place for the center of the contemplated new township must of necessity then have been a matter of speculation. It is true, our ancestors in locating a township first sought for an eligible location for a meeting-house, and an indispensable requisite for such location was high land. True to these instincts, the committee that located the first road in Tolland, and laid off the first lots to settlers, commenced upon the highest ground that then was supposed to be nearest the center of the contemplated town. As I have already said, the north line of the town of Coventry was then unknown, but was then and for many years thereafter claimed by the Windsor men to be one mile further south than it was finally found to be. There can therefore be no doubt that the first location of highways and lots in Tolland was made upon Grant's hill, and not upon the hill where the village is now located. This locality answers the description in the record. The course of the road now on Grant's hill is generally north and south, and it crosses the brook that runs up out of Cedar Swamp, and the only such brook in Tolland. The name "meeting house hill," was doubtless given to it because it was intended for the center of the new town, which could not even be regarded as a town without containing a meeting-house. But we are able to make this thing certain by the following facts which are conclusive upon this point. The record before spoken of shows that several lots of forty acres each were, by the committee who laid out this road, located on each side of it, and were granted to particular individuals. The survey of one of those lots is in these words, copied from the record aforesaid :—

The seventh lot is by the committee bounded east by the "highway; south on the sixth lot; west on undivided lands; north on the eighth lot; and containing forty acres, being in breadth forty rods north and south, and runs from the street one hundred and sixty rods west. This lot is by the committee granted to Joseph Rockwell, Jun."

The sixth lot described in this record was by this committee granted to Noah Grant, and the eighth to Thomas Grant.

On the first book of records of lands of the town of Tolland, at page seventy-nine, I find a record of a deed of land from Joseph Rockwell of Windsor, in the county of Hartford, to John Abbott, of Andover, in the county of Essex and commonwealth of Massachusetts, blacksmith; dated March 14, 1719–20, which land in said deed is described as follows:

"My dwelling house and house lot in the township of Tolland, said lot containing forty acres, being forty rods in breadth, and one hundred and threescore rods in length, be it more or less, butting and bounding west upon my own land lately set out to me by the committee of the town of Tolland in our first division of land, together with all the divisions of lands appertaining to or belonging to said home-lot, of forty acres, bounding easterly on the town highway, and south on the home-lot of Noah Grant, and north by lands firstly belonging to Thomas Grant, Jun., of Windsor, but now in possession of Nathaniel Wallis."

John Abbott the first was the great grandfather of Mrs. Sally Bliss, the wife and afterwards the widow of John Bliss,

Esq., late of Tolland, deceased. It is a traditionary fact in the family of Mr. Abbott, who is now lineally represented in Tolland in the person of Mrs. Lucius S. Fuller, that he came from Andover, Essex county, Mass., to the town of Tolland in 1720; that he bought lands of Joseph Rockwell of Windsor, that he lived in Tolland from 1720 to the day of his death, Nov. 25, 1779, then in the eighty-fifth year of his age; and that he owned the farm and lived in the house lately owned and occupied by Alfred Young, now in the possession and occupancy of James A. Brown, situated on Grant's hill. It follows that the place now occupied by Mr. James A. Brown was the place where John Abbott lived and died; was by him purchased of Joseph Rockwell, to whom the same was granted by the committee who located the first road in Tolland on meeting-house hill, and that this place is bounded easterly on that road. The meeting-house hill, named in the first record in Tolland, is now Grant's hill.

This committee made other locations and allotments of lands on the 3d day of March, and 6th day of April, 1714, which were also duly recorded,—a copy of this record was taken from the records of Windsor, August 6, 1719, certified by the committee, Matthew Allyn, Roger Wolcott, and Timothy Thrall, and was recorded in the records of lands in the town of Tolland, November 19, 1719. The entry in Tolland records is certified as follows: "November 19, 1719. I, Joseph Benton, received the foregoing record and accordingly it was recorded by me. Joseph Benton, town clerk."

The first movement towards an act of incorporation for the town was made in the year 1713. The earliest record is under date of May 9, 1713, and is in the words and figures following, viz.:

"*To the Honorable the General Assembly in Hartford, May 14, 1713.*

The petition of us the subscribers humbly showeth: That whereas your petitioners being inhabitants of this colony, and the descendants of those that have for a long time contributed to the support of the same, being through the numerous increase of our families much straitened for want of land whereon to make improvement and get our livelihood:

and being encouraged by your honors' wonted goodness to encourage the settling of plantations in the waste lands within the colony, and having viewed a township of land on the east side of the great river, ordered by the town of Windsor and the heirs of Mr. Thomas Burnham, deceased, to be settled into a plantation bounded as in their agreement doth fully appear;—many of us having already been out with the committee and taken up lots in the same, and shall with those that are desirous to settle with us, speedily settle a fair town there if the government discourage us not; we therefore humbly pray your honors would grant that a township may be made of said land, and that they may be patented to and holden by such inhabitants as shall be admitted by the committee appointed by the town of Windsor, and heirs of Mr. Thomas Burnham, deceased, and your petitioners shall ever pray." Dated, May 9, 1713.

This petition is signed by the following persons, viz.:

Baker, Joseph	Grant, Samuel	Porter, Nathaniel
Barber, Benjamin	Grant, Noah	Porter, Joseph
Birge, Cornelius	Grant, Nathaniel	Rockwell, Joseph
Bissell, Josiah	Gridley, John	Rockwell, Samuel
Chapman, Henry	Hoskins, Anthony	Stiles, Thomas
Chapman, Simon	Holcomb, Benaiah	Stiles, Henry, Jr.
Cook, Nathaniel	Huntington, John	Skinner, Joseph
Cook, Ebenezer	Loomer, H.	Stoughton, Israel
Cook, Daniel	Loomis, Stephen	Smith, Philip
Drake, Nathaniel	Loomis, Ichabod	Wolcott, Roger
Eno, John	Loomis, David	Watson, Nathaniel
Ellsworth, Samuel	Loomis, Joshua	Wolcott, Charles
Edgar, Thomas	Marshall, 'amuel	Wolcott, Henry
Eggleston, Thomas	Mills, Jedidiah	Willes, Joshua, Sen.
Farnsworth, Joseph	Phelps, Joseph	Willes, John
Gillett, Cornelius	Phelps, William	Willes, Joshua
Gaylord, Jonas	Pinney, Humphrey	Willes, Samuel
Griswold, Daniel, Jr.	Pinney, Jonathan	Warren, Robert
Gillett, Nathaniel, Jr.	Pinney, Nathaniel	Loomis, Daniel.
Griswold, Thomas	Porter, Daniel	59 in all.

The next movement was at the General Assembly in May, 1715, when the following petition was presented:

"To the Honorable the General Assembly sitting at Hartford, May 12, 1715: The petition of the town of Windsor humbly showeth:—That your petitioners did in the year 1636, purchase of the Indians certain lands on the east side of Windsor; and since the town has immeasurably increased and many inhabitants forced to seek after new settlements, and the town did in conjunction with the heirs of Mr. Thomas Burnham release their claims to said lands unto such sober inhabitants as should orderly settle on the same, paying only the prime cost; and therefore several sober and religious persons viewing the same, are very desirous to settle the same, *and several families are already there*, giving a fair prospect of a likely town—if this Honorable Assembly would graciously grant a town there, and the land to be holden by such as shall orderly settle on the same: which we pray this Honorable Assembly would graciously do; and we beg leave further to move them thereto by the following considerations:

1. The Assembly hath hitherto done the like on like occasions, and it hath been found the best way to settle the country quietly;—

2. Our purchase was improved before his Majesty for obtaining the colony patent, and he by it moved thereby to grant the lands to the colony:—Therefore we pressing the same arguments to the Assembly, hope to find the same favor;—

3. It is most reasonable the ancient inhabitants who have supported the colony should by the government be allowed to settle the lands before strangers and without paying excessive prices to all pretenders, which hath led us into all imaginable confusion already.

And your petitioners shall ever pray."

"At a town meeting in Windsor, March 21, 1714-15—It was voted: that the above written petition should be preferred to the General Assembly in May with their desire it may be granted. Test, John Moore, Register."

This petition is now on file in the archives of the state at Hartford, and at the Assembly in May, 1715, the following resolution was passed.

"And it is further resolved by this Assembly upon the petition of Windsor men that they shall, after the regulation of Coventry according to the foregoing act of this Assembly, have a township of six miles square laid out to them which shall be called Tolland, bounded on the south with Coventry, and east with Willimantic river; and in case the claimers mentioned in the preceding act shall pay in proportion to what is in the said act settled with respect to Coventry, and also by their inhabitants therein seated by Windsor committee as in the aforesaid act is provided for the like quantity of land, the said inhabitants settled by Windsor committee to pay all the charges of laying out and settling the said land,—that a quitclaim of this governments claim shall also be in like manner executed by the Governor and Secretary and delivered to the claimers, for the claim of this government for so much of the said township as shall fall within the bounds of the said claimers. And it is further resolved that a quitclaim of this governments right shall also be executed in like manner by the Governor and Secretary to Col. Matthew Allyn, and Roger Wolcott Esqr., Timothy Thrall and John Ellsworth all of Windsor, in trust for themselves and such others as shall by them be admitted to settle in said township, for all that part of said township *that lieth without the bounds of said proprietors claims as aforesaid.* Provided the said Allyn and others do pay to the public treasury of this colony for the said land in proportion to what is in this act before stated in respect of Coventry; and it is further provided that none of the claims in the foregoing act shall be construed to oblige any of the aforesaid inhabitants seated on any of the said lands, who have procured the claims of the said proprietors and have instruments under their hands to show for the same, and it is also to be understood and it is hereby resolved that the said proprietors if need be, shall give further and better assurance to the said inhabitants to whom the said proprietors have sold their claims and received the money for the same. Provided also, that the above mentioned claimers do or shall well and truly pay or cause to be paid into the colony treasury the aforesaid sum or sums on or before the 15th day of May next, or else they shall not claim the benefit of this act, any thing herein contained to the contrary notwithstanding."

By this resolution, the Windsor men became entitled to a township six miles square, to be bounded south on Coventry, and east on Willimantic river, and to be called Tolland. The fee of this territory was to be vested in Matthew Allyn, Roger Wolcott, Timothy Thrall and John Ellsworth in trust for themselves, and for such others as should by them be admitted to settle in the township. These gentlemen, it will be perceived, were the committee who located the first highway, and made the first allotments in Tolland, April 18, 1713. These trustees, on the 11th day of May, 1719, conveyed by deed of that date, the north part of Tolland to fifty-one persons named in said deed; the portion of land conveyed in said deed was described as follows:—

"Bounded south on a line east and west at the south end of Shenups pond, east on Willimantic river, and is to be in length from Willimantic river west six miles, and in breadth is from said line drawn east and west at the south end of Shenups pond so far north as to make the six miles from Coventry north bounds."

The following are the names of the grantees in this deed:

Baker,	Eaton, Daniel	Paulk, Samuel
Benton, Samuel, Sen.	Ellsworth, Jonathan	Porter, Hezekiah
Benton, Samuel, Jun.	Ellsworth, John	Porter, Daniel
Benton, Joseph, Sen.	Forward, Samuel	Rockwell, Samuel
Benton, Joseph, Jun.	Gillett, Nathan	Royce, Joseph
Birge, Cornelius	Grant, Noah	Rockwell, Joseph, Jun.
Bissell, Ephraim's heirs	Grant, Nathaniel	Stearns, Shubael
Birge, Joseph	Hatch, Joseph	Stoughton, Thomas
Brace, Stephen	Hinsdale, Barnabas	Taylor, Nathaniel
Cook, Daniel	Huntington, Christopher	Tucker, Ephraim
Coy, Samuel	Huntington, John	Utley, Samuel
Chapman, Simon	Loomis, Enoch	Wolcott, Henry
Caswell, Matthew	Loomis, Moses	Wolcott, Simon
Drake, Joseph	Loomis, Joshua	Wallis, Nathaniel
Ellis, Thomas	Nye, Ebenezer	West, Samuel
Emmons, Peter	Pinney, Samuel	Willes, Joshua
Eaton, William	Peck, Joseph	Whipple, Thomas.

I can not find any record of the original title of the southern part of the town before the year 1718, of which I shall by and by speak. There can be no doubt it was, by some conveyance, vested in the committee who commenced making the allotments in April, 1713. The petition of the town of Windsor contains an allegation that the town did " in the year 1636 purchase of the Indians certain lands on the east side of Windsor," and " did in conjunction with the heirs of Mr. Thomas Burnham, release their claims to said lands unto such sober inhabitants as should orderly settle the same;" which clearly evinces the fact that some portion of the territory contained in the proposed township had already been the subject of a conveyance. And the resolution of the General Assembly authorized the conveyance to Matthew Allyn and his associates only so much of the land that was within the six miles square " *that lieth without the bounds of said proprietors claims as aforesaid.*" It is therefore obvious that the title to the south part of Tolland was originally derived from the Indians, and it was the source of bitter controversies during the early settlement of the town. From what tribe of Indians this title was obtained, does not appear. Before the settlement at Windsor in 1633, the territory now embraced in the State of Connecticut was inhabited and probably owned by several small Indian tribes. But the boundaries between these tribes were never very well defined, and indeed, in some instances, different tribes claimed the same land, and the early settlers not unfrequently received deeds of the same land from different sachems or Indian chiefs. That portion of Connecticut situated east of Connecticut river was inhabited and owned by the following Indian tribes, to wit: The Pequots, who were located between the Niantic and Paucatuc rivers, and extending from the shore back into the country. The Mohegans, supposed to be a branch of the Pequots, whose principal town was between New London and Norwich, but whose territory extended north into the southern part of Tolland county. The Nehantics of Lyme, and the Podunks of East Windsor and East Hartford. The Nipmucs of Massachusetts had a few sparse settlements in the northern portion of Tolland and Windham counties. The town of Windsor, on the west side of the river, was subject to the Tunxis, a tribe that inhabited the valley of Farmington river. As I have said, it nowhere appears from which of these tribes the settlers at Windsor purchased lands on the east side of Windsor in 1636, for it is probable that the Mohegans, the Podunks, and the Nipmucs might have each claimed the territory. Whatever may have been the claims of others, it is certain the Mohegans regarded a portion of the territory now included within the boundaries of Tolland as their own, and hence we find that one of their sachems named Joshua, as early as the year 1675, undertook to dispose of it by will,—as by the following extract from the record of it will appear.

"Item. I give and bequeath all that tract of land lying from the mountain in sight of Hartford northward to a pond called Shenups, east to Willimantic river, south by said river, west by Hartford bounds, (except three hundred acres already sold to Major John Talcott, and two hundred acres to Capt. Thomas Bull, and according to a draught or map drawn and subscribed with my own hand, bearing date with these presents,) viz.: to Mr. James Richards, Mr. Samuel Wyllys, Capt. Thomas Bull, Mr. Joseph Haynes, Mr. Richard Lord, Major John Talcott, Mr. John Allyn, Mr. Ebenezer Way, Bartholomew Barrett, Nicholas Olmsted, Henry Hayward, Mr. Joseph Fitch, Thomas Burnham, and William Pitkin, to be equally divided amongst them, into so many parts as there are persons, and also Nathaniel Willett to have an equal proportion amongst them. Dated at Pettupaug 29 Feb. 1675. Compared Feb. 8, 1686. John Allyn, Secry."

This will describes that portion of the town of Tolland not included in the deed of Matthew Allyn and others, and is that part of the town where the first surveys were made by the proprietors' committee. I have no evidence that this tract of land was ever divided among the legatees according to the provisions of the will, and probably it never was. The Thomas Burnham named in this will, was doubtless the Thomas Burnham whose heirs united with the town of Windsor in releasing their claims to the territory of Tolland " unto such sober inhabitants as should orderly settle the same," and hence the first settlers had whatever right was vested in Windsor by virtue of their purchase of the Indians in 1636, and also the right Thomas Burnham acquired under the will of Joshua. But the legatees of Joshua were dissatisfied with the action of the first settlers, and prosecuted them for trespassing upon their rights. The settlers resisted this claim of the legatees, and made it one common cause, defraying all necessary expenses from the common treasury of the proprietors of the township. The first suit was commenced in April, 1724, by one Joseph Baker against one Shubael Stearns. In September, 1724, the proprietors, at a meeting held for that purpose, appointed Francis West, Daniel Eaton, and Shubael Stearns a committee to agree with the claimants, " with power to go to the General Court at New Haven." It appears that this committee attended the General Court at New Haven, where a committee was appointed " to treat with the proprietors of Tolland." This controversy was of great importance to the proprietors, and no doubt very seriously affected the early settlement of the town. It extended to a very large portion of the land included in their charter and went to the validity of their title. After various conferences between the committee above named, the matter was finally compromised, and the General Assembly, at its session in October, 1724, passed an act that the proprietors of Tolland should pay to the legatees of Joshua at the rate of six pounds per allotment, or three shillings per acre for the land, and that the legatees should release all their title to said lands. This action of the General Court was not acceptable to the legatees and they seemed unwilling thus to give up their claims;—and as late as October, 1728, or four years after the decision of the General Court above-mentioned, other suits were commenced upon the same claims. The proprietors held a meeting, October 28, 1678, and chose a committee consisting of Dea. Francis West, Capt. Hope Lathrop, Lieut. John Huntington, Sergeant Samuel Benton, and Sergeant Samuel Chapman, " to go to the legatees of Joshua and in the name and behalf of the proprietors to take a quitclaim deed of all their claims to the lands in Tolland." They also solemnly obligated themselves " to pay all such sums as said committee should be compelled to pay in the business of their office." This committee promptly attended to the business assigned them, and in a few months obtained proper conveyances from the legatees of Joshua which put an end to this expensive and important controversy.

It is a matter of some doubt at what precise time the first settlement was made in Tolland. The opinion generally prevails that the first permanent settlement was in 1715, but I am satisfied it was at an earlier date. It is certain that roads were laid out, and allotments of lands made to individuals in April, 1713. Tradition informs us that the persons who executed this work provided themselves with a temporary home, under a large shelving rock, now situated on the west side of the highway, leading to Bolton, near the north bank of the brook that runs across the road this side of the present residence of Alden B. Crandall. The walls of the dwelling, as well as the roof, being of stone, it received the name of Stoney house; and this gave name to the brook that runs by it, which is in the early records of the town called Stoney house brook. While it is probable that the residence of persons at this place was temporary, yet there are several facts tending to show that permanent settlements were commenced in about 1713. The petition to the General Assembly for an act of incorporation, dated May 9, 1713, alleges that many of the petitioners " have been out with the committee and have taken up lots in the same;

and shall with those that are desirous to settle with us *speedily* settle a fair town there," &c. The petition of the town of Windsor for the same object, alleges " that several families are already there, giving a fair prospect of a likely town," &c. This petition is dated March 21, 1714–15. The resolution of the General Assembly under date of May, 1715, speaks of the inhabitants thereon seated by the Windsor committee;—from all which it is evident there must have been settlements in Tolland before May, 1715. And further, in the records of the marriages, births and deaths in the town, we find the records of several births in Tolland, prior to May, 1715. The earliest of them is that of Amy Hatch, a daughter of Joseph Hatch, who was born October 10, 1713. Margaret Pack, a daughter of Joseph Pack, was born January 7, 1715 ; Joseph Hatch, son of Joseph Hatch before mentioned, and as tradition says the first male child born in Tolland, was born Sept. 12, 1715. Joseph Pack had land assigned him in the early allotments, and his name and that of Joseph Hatch are among the earliest upon the records. From these facts I am confident the first settlement in Tolland must have been made in the year 1713.

There is no positive evidence that the territory within the limits of Tolland was ever occupied by the Indians, other than for hunting and fishing. Formerly our ponds and streams were stored with excellent fish, and our forests were filled with a great variety of wild game, which during certain portions of the year invited the attention of the savage inhabitants occupying the land near the sea-shore. I have myself heard some of the aged people say, they had seen shad and salmon caught in large quantities in Willimantic river, between Tolland and Willington, and so plentifully were salmon caught, that fishermen had a standing rule that they would not sell a certain number of shad to one person unless he would take a certain quantity of salmon. The Indians in their summer visits to this town, found it necessary or convenient to erect wigwams or Indian huts,—traces of which in the western part of the town, on lands lately owned by Mr. Ephraim West and Mr. Timothy Benton, were visible within the recollection of some of our oldest inhabitants. A few families may have occupied these huts, but they left the town before its first settlement and none of the red men have ever dwelt here since. We have but few objects to which any Indian name was ever known to be attached. The Indians gave the name of Wangombog to a large portion of country in the southern part of Tolland county, adjacent to the large pond known by this name, situated in the town of Coventry. A portion of the town of Tolland was within the territory called Wangombog, and several of the early deeds recorded in Tolland, describe the land conveyed as situated in Wangombog. The same name is given to the locality of the land conveyed in the will of Joshua, before mentioned. The pond on the west side of Tolland, was by the Indians called Shenipset, which by an easy corruption is now pronounced Snipsic. This word is variously spelled in the old records—sometimes Shenipset, Shenaps, Shenips.

The small stream running east of the village was by the Indians called Skungamug—the corruption of which is Skunkamug or Skunkermug—sometimes in the old records written Scungamuck. These Indian names, though less euphonious than some of our more modern ones, I hope will be perpetuated. Indeed, I entertain some doubt whether they will sound any more harsh in the ears of our posterity than Ball Hill, Sugar Hill, Buff Cap, Goose Lane, or Cedar Swamp—all of which are the recognized modern names of well-known localities.

As I have already intimated, there was early a difficulty about the true location of the north line of the town of Coventry. The Windsor proprietors, under date of May 14, 1716, petitioned for a "final settlement with the legatees of Joshua; for setting of bounds with the town of Coventry, concerning which there is much difficulty;" also, "that we may have privilege to choose a town clerk and other officers as the law directs." This petition purports to be the petition "of us the subscribers, inhabitants of Tolland," and was negatived by the Assembly. The following are the names of the petitioners, to wit:

Baker, Joseph	Ellis, Thomas	Stearns, Shubael
Benton, Joseph	Grant, Nathaniel	Willes, Joshua
Birge, Cornelius	Loomis, Joshua	Wolcott, Henry
Benton, Samuel	Mather, Joseph	Taylor, Nathaniel.
Bradley, George	Porter, Hezekiah	16 in all.
Bissell, Ephraim	Porter, Joseph	

In May, 1718, a petition was presented to the General Assembly, as follows, to wit: "A petition of us the subscribers, inhabitants of Tolland, relative to Coventry lands." Signed by the following persons:

Baker, Joseph	Loomis, Joshua	Slafter, Joseph
Birge, Cornelius	Loomis, Enoch	Slafter, Antony
Benton, Joseph	Nye, Ebenezer	Stimpson, James
Benton, Daniel	Pack, Joseph	Stoughton, Thomas
Cook, Daniel	Porter, Hezekiah	Taylor, Nathaniel
Drake, Joseph	Porter, Joseph	Willes, Joshua
Eaton, William	Rice, Joseph	Wolcott, Simon.
Grant, Noah	Rockwell, Joseph	25 in all.
Hatch, Joseph	Stearns, Shubael	

I am unable to ascertain at what time the line between Tolland and Coventry was finally settled, but I have no doubt it was done before 1720, in which year a committee appointed by the General Assembly, located the town of Tolland and defined its boundaries. The following is a copy of their report:

"This may certify whom it may concern, that we, James Wadsworth and John Hall, on this   day of October, A. D. 1720, being assisted by Thomas Kimberly, surveyor and in company with sundry men of the town of Tolland, did pursuant to an act of the General Assembly of this colony, held at Hartford May 12, 1720, survey and lay out the north and west bounds of the town of Tolland; and for that end we went to the north-east corner of the town of Coventry; and from thence due north (by the needle of the instrument,) six miles, at the end whereof to wit, in an east line by the needle, at or on the west bank of Willimantic river, we erected a heap of stones for the north-east corner of the township of Tolland, and marked a red oak tree on the south side with the letter T; and from thence ran upon a point west (by the needle,) six miles seventeen rods and thirteen links to a white oak tree marked and a heap of stones about it, standing on the southerly side of a hill, which tree is the north-west corner boundary of said Tolland; and from the said tree to run south, five degrees west to Coventry north-west corner;—the land contained within the said town lines, and the said river which is the east bounds of said town is of the contents of six miles square. The chainmen were under oath as the law directed.

A true copy of record. (Signed,) JAMES WADSWORTH.
Examined by Hez. Wyllys, Sec'y.   JOHN HALL."

From this certificate it is very evident that the north line of Coventry was substantially settled before October, 1720, and became the basis of the action of the above-named committee in locating the north and west lines of the town of Tolland. But there were subsequent negotiations between these towns upon this subject. The towns of Coventry and Tolland appointed a committee of three from each town to agree about the dividing line, and they were empowered to make a final issue and determination of the lines between the towns. This committee consisted of Samuel Parker, Joseph Strong and Thomas Root, of Coventry; and Joseph Hatch, Daniel Eaton and Noah Grant, of Tolland, and met on the 6th day of February, 1722, and agreed that the dividing line between the two towns should be the line run by Capt. James Wadsworth, Capt. John Hall, and Mr. Kimberly, and that the same should thereafter be perambulated according to law. They further agreed, " that Francis West and Joseph Benton, being in Coventry, might pay their public dues in Tolland, with three acres of land a-piece about their houses, and counted inhabitants of Tolland, as if Tolland had took them in; they and their heirs and assigns living on the three acres of land where their houses now stand." Francis West found it impracticable to reside in one town and exercise town privileges in another, and he very soon removed his house from Coventry to Tolland. This house is the one lately occupied by Billaky Snow, now deceased.

It would seem that the settlement with the legatees of Joshua, and the establishment of the line between the towns of Coventry and Tolland, might sufficiently quiet all conflicting claims and remove all doubts respecting the corporate powers of the town of Tolland and the title of its inhabitants to the territory within the limits of its charter. But lest there might be some defect in the previous proceedings, or some omission which might cause further difficulties, the town procured from the General Assembly, at its session in New Haven, October, 1728, the passage of a resolution confirming and establishing every thing that had been previously done. This resolution, after reciting the resolution of May 12, 1715, recognizes the survey made by Messrs. Wadsworth and Hall in 1720, and also the deed to the proprietors of Tolland, dated May 11, 1719, and then declares that the proprietors " held the lands of the said township as one entire propriety; and that all the said proprietors shall have equal interest and benefit by force of the patent by the said assembly granted to be executed to the said proprietors in usual form."

In pursuance with this resolution a patent was issued by the Governor, countersigned by the Secretary of State, dated the 2d day of Nov., 1728, in and by which all the powers, privileges and franchises before granted to the Windsor men, were ratified and confirmed, and the title to the land within the boundaries of the town as described by the survey of Messrs. Wadsworth and Hall, was fully, clearly, absolutely given, granted, ratified and confirmed unto Henry Wolcott, Stephen Steel, Francis West, together with the rest of the proprietors of the town; and to their heirs and assigns, and such as should thereafter legally succeed to, and represent them forever in such proportion as they the said proprietors, partners and settlers, or any of them respectively had right in, or were lawfully possessed of the same. Also authorizing and empowering said proprietors and inhabitants of said town, from time to time, and at all times forever thereafter, to exercise and enjoy all such rights, powers, privileges and franchises in and among themselves, as were given, granted, allowed and exercised and enjoyed by and amongst the proprietors of other towns of the colony, according to the common approved custom and observance; and guaranteeing to said grantees, their heirs and assigns legally representing them, " a good, pure, perfect, absolute and indefeasible estate of inheritance, in fee simple, in the lands described, to be holden of his majesty his heirs and successors, as of his majesty's manor of East Greenwich in the county of Kent in the Kingdom of England, in free and common socage, and not in capite nor by knight service, yielding therefor and paying unto our sovereign lord king George, his heirs and successors forever, one fifth part of all ore of gold and silver, which from time to time and at all times forever thereafter, shall be there gotten, had or obtained in lieu of all services, dutys and demands whatsoever."

NOTE. Socage, is a tenure by any certain and determinate service. It is of two kinds—Free socage, and villein socage. Free socage is when the services are not only certain but honorable. Villien socage is where the services, though certain, are of a degraded nature. The tenure by which the lands granted in the foregoing patent were holden, was one-fifth part of all ore of gold and silver found within the limits of the town. This was both certain and honorable, and in the absence of these precious metals will never be a great burden to the inhabitants of that town.

MEETING-HOUSES.

THE first settlers of Tolland exhibited a very strong attachment to religious institutions. Being lineal descendants of that band of pilgrims that left their native land, to seek across the trackless waters an asylum where they could worship the God of their fathers unmolested, according to the dictates of their own consciences, it is not strange that they should regard the social organization as entirely imperfect without a spiritual leader to break to them the bread of life. A minister and a house for public worship were not only regarded by them as essential to their happiness, but as indispensable to their worldly prosperity; and hence all sacrifices necessary to the attainment of these objects were most cheerfully made. The early records of the town furnish conclusive evidence of their intense zeal upon this subject, and their great liberality in a cause so near their hearts. They were authorized by the General Assembly to choose town officers in the year 1717, and the first town clerk and selectmen were chosen in that year. In the year 1719, when probably there were not over twenty-five families in town, a vote was passed appropriating eighty acres of land for a minister lot, and offering a salary of seventy-five pounds, or two hundred and fifty dollars a year, making an average sum of ten dollars annually to each family. On the 19th day of November, 1719, the proprietors of the town voted to build a meeting-house, thirty feet square, and appointed Noah Grant, William Eaton, and Joseph Benton, a committee " to order the affairs of the meeting-house."

There was, as usual, some difficulty in locating this house; and the records show that several meetings were held on the subject, which served to delay the building of the house for several months. The spot where it was finally erected was agreed upon February 5, 1721–22; which was on the hill a little east of the present residence of Mr. William West. At a previous meeting held on the 31st of January, 1720–1, the town voted to build a meeting-house thirty feet long and twenty-eight feet wide, with eighteen feet posts. They also voted that the frame of the building should be raised by the last day of the month of June next following, and that the sides should be covered, and the floors laid, and windows put in, by the last of the following November. It is not probable that any very serious effort was made to comply with these votes; for I find the record of a town meeting held on the first of May of the same year, at which it was voted that the building should be forty-five feet long, thirty-five feet wide, and twenty feet between joints. As this is the last vote upon the subject of dimensions, it is fair to presume that the house was finally built as last prescribed, and was probably raised in the spring of 1722. It does not appear when this house was dedicated to the worship of God, yet there can be no doubt public worship was held in it early in the year 1723.

October 4, 1725, a tax of four pence on the pound was laid to defray the expenses "arisen and arising about furnishing the meeting-house." February 28, 1726, it was voted to build pews upon that part of the floor that was raised above the rest. December, 1728, it was voted "to build a house about twenty feet by fourteen, near the meeting-house, to accommodate the inhabitants living remote from the meeting-house with a place to spend the intermission between services without troubling others." December 9, 1730, the town voted that "the selectmen should procure at the towns cost what is necessary for the pulpit." December 8, 1731, it was voted " to do something towards repairing and finishing the galleries." From 1744 to 1749, liberty was given divers persons to "erect pews in the galleries at their own expense and for their own accommodation."

It would seem that this house did not answer the purpose for which it was designed; for we find that before it had stood thirty years, to wit, on the 28th of January, 1751, the town, by a vote of nearly two to one, voted " that it was necessary to build a new meeting-house for public worship in said town." The question of building a new meeting-house at this time, must have been one of unusual interest, for at this meeting we find that no less than twenty-eight persons were admitted inhabitants of the town, and one hundred and ten votes were given upon the question, viz., seventy in the affirmative, and forty in the negative. Three unsuccessful attempts were made to rescind this vote, but the town adhered with increased majorities each time to its first decision. The location of this house was a matter of even more than usual interest. The inhabitants of the north-west and western portions of the town insisted upon a site at the north end of the street, while those of the southern and eastern portions were equally strenuous for its location at the south end of the street. The matter was at first submitted to the town, and a majority of votes decided in favor of the southern location. There was then no road leading into the street from the eastern part of the town, except the one leading from near where the old meeting-house stood, and of course all persons attending meetings from the eastern part of the town would have to come into the street at the south end, which doubtless had its influence in determining the location of the house. Tradition says that the influence of the Hon. Zebulon West, whose residence was in the south part of the town, had great weight in the final settlement of this question. The minority did not readily submit to the decision of the majority, and they appealed to the General Court and obtained a committee to review the proceedings of the town, but after several public hearings, the location fixed by vote of the town was finally confirmed. On the 24th day of December, 1753, the town voted to build the new meeting-house fifty-six feet long and forty feet wide. This house was raised in the month of May, 1754, and was so far finished as to be used for public worship in the Spring of 1755. The house was erected without a steeple, and it was not until the year 1792, that the town came to the conclusion not to dispense with this appendage any longer. At a town meeting held on the 12th day of January, 1792, they voted " That the town will build a steeple to the meeting-house, Provided, that a bell can be procured and given to the town without burdening the town with any expense for said bell." The bell was to be procured by voluntary subscription, and such progress was made in this direction, that the town, at an adjourned meeting on the second day of February, 1792, voted " to raise a tax on the last August list two pence and one farthing on the pound to build a steeple to the meeting-house in Tolland." It is a traditional fact, that the inhabitants of the north-west and western portions of the town were very much opposed to the project of building the steeple, and it is said that two persons, viz., Gen. Chapman, and his uncle, Simon Chapman, were the only persons from that quarter of the town who voted in the affirmative on this question. It is also said that the old feud growing out of the location of the meeting-house was fully revived and had its effect upon those who voted in the negative. It seems the people were hardly satisfied with the action of the town on this subject, and another town meeting was called as will appear by the following vote copied from the town records under date of April 26, 1792:

"Voted at said meeting that the town consider the first article in the warning for a town meeting at this time first, (viz.) whether they will reconsider the vote passed at a former town meeting to build a steeple to the meeting-house. Voted, to take that up first. The question was then put whether the town would reconsider their vote passed at a former meeting to build a steeple to the meeting-house. Negatived by the whole."

The following vote furnishes some evidence that the old difficulty about the location of the house was not entirely forgotten. It is under date of May 4, 1792, and is as follows, to wit:

"Voted to choose an agent to send to Hartford to attend the General Assembly at the present session to oppose the memorial of a number of inhabitants of the town of Tolland, referred to said Assembly, praying for liberty to move the meeting-house in said Tolland to some other place near the centre of said town."

It is probable that the steeple was built and the bell procured and in use before December 3d, 1792, for on that day a town meeting was held at which the following votes were passed :

Voted, "That a tax of one penny, three farthings on the pound be laid and collected on the last August grand list, to pay up the committee the residue of their bills for building the steeple to the meeting-house; and the overplus, if any, to remain to defray other town expenses. At the same meeting, Voted, That the selectmen of said town procure Mr. Hanks to run over the bell, if he will do it on reasonable terms, and to hang it again in the steeple."

Mr. Hope Lathrop, an influential citizen, was very active in procuring subscriptions for the bell. It is said he went into the west part of the town to obtain funds for this purpose, and being universally refused, he became a little excited, and declared that those who would not give anything for the bell should not hear it ring.

The collection of the tax for building the steeple was resisted by people in the western part of the town, and the collector, under the direction of the selectmen, distrained an ox, the property of Nathaniel Kingsbury, Jr., to pay his tax. This Nathaniel Kingsbury was an elder brother of Deacon Jabez Kingsbury, whose grand-children still own and live on the farm owned by him during his life time. Mr. Nathaniel Kingsbury brought an action against Daniel Edgerton and others, then selectmen of Tolland, to test the legality of this tax. The writ was dated January 28, 1793; the facts were agreed to by the parties, and the cause was carried to the Supreme Court of Errors. Two questions were made in the case:—1. That the town had no right to tax its inhabitants to build a steeple to its meeting-house; and 2. If it had this right it could only be exercised by a vote of two-thirds of the voters at a legal meeting; and inasmuch as the tax in question was laid by a majority vote only, it was not legally laid.

But the court ruled both questions in favor of the town, and the plaintiff had to pay the costs.

Tradition informs us that the first public use to which the first bell was put, was tolling for the death of Capt. Hope Lathrop, who was so active in procuring it, and that it was cracked on that occasion. He died November 8, 1792, and the meeting, to have Mr. Hanks recast the bell, was held December 3, 1792; a fact that corroborates the traditional evidence.

NOTE. The steeple built by the town of Tolland in 1792, was just one hundred feet high, and was the first or nearly the first ever built in the county. It, of course, attracted great attention, and was scrutinized by people from other towns. One Oliver Arnold, happening in Tolland, and knowing somewhat of the difficulties respecting the building of the steeple, stood gazing upon it, when a sort of inspiration came upon him, and he gave vent to his reflections in the following doggerel:

"Poor Tolland; grand people!
Old meeting house, and new steeple!"

This doggerel distich has more meaning than at first sight is apparent. It not only exhibits the envious feelings of the speaker towards the people of Tolland, but contains a sarcastic criticism upon their conduct. The term "poor Tolland," was intended to describe the pecuniary condition of the town, as exhibited in its barren hills and broken land. The term "grand people," was used to express the contempt which the speaker felt for the distinguishing characteristics of the town as the county metropolis. The people had just built a court-house, jail, and a tall steeple. The other line is a biting criticism on the taste and judgment of the people in having an old building to meet in with a new steeple for ornament.

Another incident will illustrate this feeling more fully. It was formerly the practice of the profession to attend the Superior Court on its circuit, and remain until the court adjourned. Many leading members of the bar, in Windham and New London counties, were in the habit of attending the courts in Tolland, and were often engaged in the more important trials. On one occasion, after a session of some interest, a gentleman from Norwich took occasion publicly to congratulate the people of Tolland on their recent improvements, and the brilliant prospects before them; and continuing his remarks with more of irony than truth, said he entertained no doubt Tolland would yet be a port of entry, and vessels would be seen unloading their cargoes upon the banks of the Skungamug. A resident of Tolland, standing by, and not much relishing the sarcasm of the speaker, interrupted him by saying that the event of which he was speaking was, in his judgment, much nearer at hand than he, the speaker, anticipated; for, said he, the *small craft* from the city of Norwich have already found their way amongst us, and their larger vessels will doubtless follow in their wake.

Although this meeting-house was so far finished as to be used for public worship in 1755, it was not entirely completed until several years afterwards, for I find a record of a vote, passed on the 3d day of March, 1760, raising a tax for finishing the meeting-house, which was made payable the first day of November then next following. The interior of this house was fitted up with square pews, having seats usually on three sides, so that a large portion of the audience had to sit with their sides or backs to the minister. These pews furnished very indifferent accommodations for worshippers who indulged in the somniferous habits of some of the present generation. The training of our ancestors, and their sense of propriety, seemed to incline them to think less of their bodily ease and comfort, during public worship, than of the manner and spirit with which it was conducted. In their day it was no particular hardship for females to walk two and three miles every sabbath to meeting, if the weather would permit; and very few were ever found in any congregation so overcome with bodily fatigue as to be unable or unwilling to stand erect during the entire devotional part of the exercises. It would doubtless have been a matter of surprise and astonishment could they have foreseen that their posterity, within half a century, would become so effeminate as to be unable to walk half a mile to attend public worship, or to stand during the singing of a short hymn.

The meeting-house, of which I have been speaking, was taken down in the summer of 1838, being eighty-four years after its erection. The meeting-house now used by the Congregational society was then built, and was publicly dedicated to religious services on the 25th day of October, 1838.

The house which belongs to the Methodist society was erected by voluntary contributions in the year 1794. Its interior was at first very rude and the seats uncomfortable. It underwent a most thorough repair in the year 1832, and by subsequent repairs and alterations has been somewhat improved. There has never been any money expended upon it from the town treasury, the whole expense having been borne by individuals. The house belonging to the Baptist denomination was built by subscription in the year 1832, and has been throughly repaired. Before the building of this house, this congregation held their meetings in the old court-house, when that edifice was standing, and afterwards in the old school-house of the Center district.

MINISTERS.

The first vote on record in Tolland, respecting ministers, is under date of June 15, 1719, and is in the following words, to wit: "At a meeting of the inhabitants of Tolland, they did choose Joseph Benton to go to see if he can get a minister to be amongst us, to preach the gospel amongst us." From sundry votes of the town, passed in the months of January and February, 1719-20, it is certain that Rev. Stephen Steel was then officiating as a clergyman in this town. On the 17th day of said February the town voted "to give the minister sixty pounds a year, and not to build him a house," and also, "that John Yeomans and Joseph Benton shall go to Mr. Stephen Steel to see if he will accept of what they have agreed to do for him." On the 22d of September, 1720, "it was voted, that Mr. West, Mr. Yeomans, Mr. Eaton and Joseph Benton shall be a committee to wait or call on Mr. Steel for a longer time to be with us; and to see whether he will settle with us." On the 7th of November "it was voted, that they will give to Mr. Steel, if he will settle amongst us, the sum of seventy-five pounds, to be paid in money or provisions, at the market price, and a lot and allottment amongst us; he settling himself in the work of the ministry amongst us." It does not distinctly appear from the records whether Mr. Steel accepted this call; but that he was the minister of the town from the year 1719, under a contract to render services, there can be no doubt. January 31, 1721, the town voted, "they would not agree with Mr. Steel no otherwise but as it was last voted, to wit: seventy-five pounds and he to build his house." They also voted, "that his salary should begin when he began to preach with us, except the time when he was wanting." In September following, a committee was appointed "to reckon with Mr. Steel to see what was paid to him, and what was behind of his due." The committee were Joseph Benton, William Eaton, Joshua Willes and Joseph Pack. It appears that there was no organized church in Tolland before the year 1722. When, or under what circumstances, the first church was gathered, can not be learned from any records of its own, nor are there any traces of its separate action to be found until the settlement of Rev. Ansel Nash as its pastor in the year 1813. But in the town records, under date of 1722, (the month being torn off,) we find the following vote: "Voted, that Joseph Benton should get a prayer put into the General Assembly for gathering a church and ordaining a minister in Tolland." I can have no doubt that this vote was passed early in the year 1722, for there is now on file in the records of this State at Hartford, a document in the words and figures following, to wit:

"To the Honorable the Governor, Council and Representatives in General Court assembled, in Hartford, May 10, 1722. The prayer of Joseph Benton, of Tolland, humbly showeth: that under the conduct of Divine Providence, and by the favor of this honorable assembly, the aforementioned town of Tolland is settled with a competent number of inhabitants; and having obtained a suitable person to preach the gospel amongst us to the good satisfaction of the inhabitants, we are desirous to enjoy the benefits of all gospel ordinances amongst us, to which end, we, as our law directs, apply ourselves to this honorable assembly for their approbation therein; and by a vote of said town, your petitioner is empowered to make his application to this honorable assembly; and your good countenance herein will be a further obligation to your petitioner ever to pray, as in duty bound.

JOSEPH BENTON.

Upon this petition the following entries are made. "Granted in the Upper House. Test, Hezekiah Wyllis, Secretary." "The prayer above granted in the Lower House. Test, Joseph Whiting, Clerk." This document establishes the following facts: First, that the vote of the town, directing Joseph Benton to get a prayer put into the general assembly for gathering a church, was passed before May 10, 1722. Second, that the town had then obtained a minister to the acceptance of the inhabitants of the town. Third, that there was then no organized church in town. Fourth, that it was the duty of the town to obtain leave of the general assembly to gather a church, so that they might enjoy gospel ordinances. Fifth, that the general assembly did grant leave to the town of Tolland to gather a church at its session in May, 1722. The next record in order I have been able to find is a town record under date of June 19, 1723, and is as follows, to wit:

"Voted, That the church hath liberty to ordain Mr. Stephen Steel pastor of a church in Tolland. Voted, That the charge of Mr. Steel's ordination be done at the expense of the town. Voted, That Noah Grant shall be one to see that provision be made for the ordination of Mr. Steel."

"Voted, That Daniel Cook shall be one to take care that provision be made for Mr. Steel's ordination."

From the foregoing documents and records it is apparent that the church of the Congregational Society in Tolland was organized between the month of May, 1722, and the month of June, 1723, but at what precise date, or who were its first officers or members can not now be accurately ascertained. The Rev. Stephen Steel, was ordained as pastor of the church and society in Tolland in 1723, but the precise date is not known. He continued to be the pastor of the church until the 21st day of December, 1758, when the connection between him and the church and society was amicably dissolved by the parties, on account of his ill health. He died in Tolland on the 4th day of December, 1759, in the 63d year of his age.

George Steel came from England, and after a few years residence in Cambridge, Mass., was one of the earliest settlers of Hartford, Conn., and was one of the forty-two Hartford soldiers who served under Captain Mason in the Pequot war. He died in 1663 at an advanced age. His farm, now a portion of the city, of immense value, was situated around the present Washington and Lafayette streets; his house stood on the latter just out of Washington street. James Steel, his son, married for his first wife Anna Bishop, of Guilford, who died in the year 1675. He afterwards married Bethiah, widow of Samuel Stocking. James Steel, the son of James and Anna Steel, and the grandson of George Steel, was born about the year 1658, and died in 1712. He married Sarah Barnard, who died his widow in 1730. STEPHEN STEEL, the son of James and Sarah Steel, and the great grandson of George Steel, was born in Hartford in the year 1696, in the house, yet standing, on the spot where George Steel first settled. He was the first minister of Tolland.

He married Ruth Porter, of Hadley, Mass. Their children were as follows:

Ruth, their daughter, was born August 30, 1722, and died February 6, 1740–41.
Stephen,   son,   "   September 29, 1724. Died October 23, 1802.
Eleazer,   "   August 2, 1726.
Elisha,   "   October 7, 1728.
Mehitabel, daughter,   "   June 6, 1733.
James,   son,   "   February 6, 1737.
John,   "   "   November 25, 1738.
Aaron,   "   "   November 1, 1744.

Ruth, the widow of Rev. Stephen Steel, died May 14, 1792, aged ninety-one.

There was also Sarah, daughter of Rev. Stephen and Ruth Steel, who was born in Hadley about the year 1730—therefore not recorded in Tolland.

The sons of Rev. Stephen Steel, except James and Aaron, married and settled in Tolland. Stephen Steel, Jun., the eldest son, married Hannah Chapman, the daughter of Capt. Samuel Chapman. Her brother Elijah was married on the same day, (May 28, 1747,) to Sarah, daughter of Rev. Stephen Steel.

The following is a record of the children of Stephen Steel, Jr., and his wife Hannah.

```
Stephen.   their son, was born July 10, 1749, and died November 26, 1750.
Hannah.    daughter,  "   November 2, 1750.
Stephen.   son,       "   August 31, 1752.
Ruth,      daughter,  "   September 17, 1755, and died December 31, 1758.
Perez,     son,       "   May 1, 1758.
Ruth,      daughter,  "   April 29, 1762, married Samuel R. Kingsbury, August 13, 1779.
Mary,      "          "   July 25, 1765, mar. Asa Howard, died November 28. 1843, aged 78.
Daniel.    son,       "   June 24, 1769.
```

Hannah, the wife of Stephen, died August 27, 1801.

This Stephen Steel was an officer of the militia and captain of the company in Tolland; and was selectman of the town for five years.

Perez Steel, the son of Stephen and Hannah Steel, married Hannah Simons, of Tolland, June 7, 1781. The following is the record of their children.

```
Lusalla, their daughter, was born May 1, 1782, and died June 14, 1782.
Aaron.     son,        "   April 16, 1783.
Lusalla.   daughter,   "   February 23, 1785.
Perez,     son,        "   April 10, 1787.
Clarissa.  daughter,   "   August 29, 1789.
Orrenda,   "           "   April 4, 1792.
Juliana,   "           "   August 23, 1794.
```

Eleazer Steel, son of Rev. Stephen Steel and his wife Ruth, married Mrs. Ann White, of Bolton, December 28, 1749. She died February 22, 1750. Eleazer Steel married, for his second wife, Ruth Chapman, daughter of Capt. Samuel Chapman, of Tolland, November 7, 1751.

The following is their family record, to wit:

```
Eleazer.   their son, was born August 20, 1753.
Ann,       daughter,   "   April 10, 1755.
Samuel.    son,        "   May 7, 1757, died in revolutionary service, 1780
Ruth,      daughter,   "   April 27, 1760, died April 23, 1775.
Joel,      son,        "   July 24, 1762, died March 18. 1778.
Ashbel.    "           "   March 15, 1765.
David,     "           "   June 29, 1767.
Jeduthan,  "           "   February 8, 1772, died September 25, 1775.
Abigail,   daughter,   "   May 5, 1774.
```

Mrs. Ruth Steel, wife of Eleazer Steel, died December 6, 1776, aged 43.

Eleazer Steel, of Tolland, and Lois Fenton, of Willington, were married May 7, 1778. He died February 26, 1799, in the 73d year of his age. He was town clerk of Tolland for nine years, from 1776 to 1784 inclusive, and was twice a representative in the General Assembly.

Ashbel Steel, the son of Eleazer and Ruth Steel, married Elizabeth, daughter of Col. Solomon Wills, of Tolland, March 26, 1789.

The following is their family record, to wit:

THE EARLY HISTORY OF TOLLAND.

Melicent Wills, their daughter, born August 9, 1790, married S. Kent, March 3, 1812.
Salmon,   son,   "   October 6, 1792, died August 22, 1823.
Seth Dwight,   "   "   March 14, 1796, died at Windsor, Ohio, September 1, 1834.
Roxey Chapman, daughter, "   March 23, 1798, married Solo. L. Griggs, December 6, 1821.
Florilla,   "   "   September 24, 1800, died October 25, 1802.
Ashbel Smith,   son,   "   December 7, 1804, died August 30, 1811.

Ashbel Steel died May 30, 1830, aged 66 years.

Elizabeth Steel died January 26, 1832.

Ashbel Steel was captain of one of the militia companies in Tolland, and was two years a selectman. He resided near the south end of Tolland street, at the corner of the road running to the western part of the town, in the house where his father lived and kept a tavern for many years. He was a kind, obliging neighbor and most excellent citizen.

Melicent Wills Steel, his daughter, married Samuel Kent, of Suffield. They had two children, viz.: Elizabeth Sophronia Kent, now a resident of this village, and James S. Kent, a resident of Richmond, Virginia.

Eleazer Steel, Jr., son of Eleazer and Ruth Steel, married Rebecca Lathrop, daughter of Hope Lathrop, December 16, 1779. The following is their family record, to wit:

Joel,   their son, was born August 14, 1782.
Eleazar,   "   "   August 22, 1784.
Jeduthan,   "   "   February 25, 1787.
Ralph,   "   "   May 8, 1789.
Ruth,   daughter,   "   January 4, 1792.
Minerva,   "   "   September 10, 1794, married Jarvis Crandal, died February 25, 1831.
Marilla,   "   "   January 16, 1797.
Sanford, son,   "   February 27, 1799, now residing in Bolton.
George,   "   "   November 4, 1801.

Mr. Eleazer Steel died June 24, 1809. Mrs. Rebecca Steel died March 3, 1806.

James Steel, son of Rev. Stephen Steel, married Abigail Huntington, daughter of John Huntington, Esq., of Tolland, January 24, 1754.

The following is their family record, viz.:

Aaron,   their son, was born October 19, 1754, died in the revolutionary army in New Jersey.
James,   "   "   October 30, 1756, died in Ellington, 1819.
Zadoc,   "   "   December 17, 1758, died in Stansted, Canada.
Samuel,   "   "   May 10, 1761.
Andrew,   "   "   December 25, 1763.
Abigail, daughter,   "   August 16, 1766.
Deborah,   "   "   December 31, 1768.

Abigail, wife of James Steel, died January, 1769. He married for his second wife, Dorothy Converse, of Stafford, September 14, 1769. Their children were:

John, their son, was born November 8, 1770, died February 4, 1772.
John,   "   "   December 31, 1772, died January 8, 1773.

Dorothy, wife of James Steel, died March 10, 1773. He

married for his third wife, Abigail Wakefield, of Weston, January 18, 1775.

Abigail, their daughter, was born November 18, 1775.

James Steel removed with his family to Ellington, in 1776, and having resided there several years, removed to Brookfield, Vermont, where his son Zadoc had commenced a settlement, and where he died at an advanced age. His second son, James, settled in Ellington, one family of whose descendants, (that of Oliver Wolcott Steel, Esq.,) continue in that town. Andrew, fifth son of James Steel, Sen., residing in Randolph, Vermont, married Elizabeth Lathrop, of Tolland, August 17, 1785.

Elisha Steel, the son of Rev. Stephen Steel, married Sarah Wolcott, of Windsor, April 26, 1758. He graduated at Yale College in 1750, was educated for the bar, located in the town of Tolland, and engaged in the practice of his profession. He was chosen a representative in the General Assembly in 1761, and was reëlected five times. He was one of the two Justices of the Peace from 1761 to 1766 inclusive. He was the first lawyer ever located in the town of Tolland, and the only one while he lived. He died August 17, 1773.

The record of his children is as follows, to wit:

Sarah, his daughter, was born April 29, 1759.
Mara, " " May 27, 1761.
Mary-ann, " " April 28, 1763.
Elisha, son, " April 30, 1765.
Roger Wolcott, " " January 19, 1768.
Mehitabel, daughter, " May 8, 1770, died August 21, 1772.

John Steel, the son of Rev. Stephen Steel, married Sarah Cobb, daughter of Dr. Samuel Cobb, December 15, 1763. The following is the record of their children, to wit:

Eunice, their daughter, was born March 19, 1767.
Sarah, " " February 25, 1769.
John, son, " June 11, 1771, died September 8, 1777.
Eleazer, " " February 27, 1774, died September 14, 1777.
Mary, daughter, " June 11, 1776.
Ruth, " " August 11, 1778.
Rachel, " " June 19, 1780.
Lovine, " " September 29, 1782.

Of the numerous descendants of the Rev. Stephen Steel, only a few now remain in Tolland, and no one bearing the name of Steel. They are to be found, however, in other families. The Chapman family furnishes several of these descendants. The widow and children of the late Col. Ashbel Chapman, the children of the late Mr. Reuben Chapman, Mr. Daniel Chapman, Mr. Elijah S. Chapman and their children, Mrs. George H. Kingsbury and her children; Miss Elizabeth S. Kent and Charles O. Benton; George M. Grant, Edwin L. Grant, Calvin Whiton and Stephen Whiton, and their children, are descendants of Rev. Stephen Steel. The family of Sanford Steel, Esq., of Bolton, and Oliver W. Steel, Esq., of Ellington, are also of the same descent.

I am unable to give any very distinct idea of the person or character of the Rev. Stephen Steel. His death occurred one hundred and one years ago last December, and none of his cotemporaries now survive. Unfortunately, he left no publication, nor does any manuscript exist from which his intellectual and literary attainments can be estimated. He once preached the annual election sermon at Hartford, but omitted to furnish a copy for publication. The fact that he was selected for this service, is evidence that he was a man of more than ordinary ability, for in his day none but clergymen of very respectable attainments were honored with this distinction. His correspondence with the town, and the satisfactory arrangements made with its agents, when his health became so much impaired as to disable him from performing the duties of his ministerial office, give unmistakable evidence of his conciliatory spirit, his disinterestedness and his unaffected piety. He had then been the sole minister of the town for nearly forty years, had commenced with it in its infancy, when it was nearly an unbroken wilderness, containing less than twenty-five families; had seen the population increase to near one thousand, and had the satisfaction of knowing there was not, at the time of his dismissal, a single dissenting worshiper in the whole number. The Rev. Dr. Williams, the immediate successor of Mr. Steel, told a friend of mine in 1827, that at the time of his settlement, and for several years thereafter, there was not a dissenter, nor the least want of unanimity on ecclesiastical affairs in the whole town. I could almost be willing to give in my adherence to the most rigid and antiquated puritanism, if I could once more see such unanimity among those who profess to be actuated by the same spirit.

The connection between the Rev. Stephen Steel and the church and society in Tolland, was dissolved by mutual consent on the 25th day of December, 1758. The town soon invited a Mr. Gideon Noble, and afterwards a Mr. Nehemiah Strong to preach as candidates for settlement. But the Rev. NATHAN WILLIAMS received a unanimous call from the town to settle in the work of the ministry in Tolland, on the 26th day of November, 1759,—they offering to pay him two hundred pounds, (six hundred sixty-six dollars and sixty-six cents,) as a settlement, and eighty pounds, (two hundred sixty six dollars, sixty-six cents,) as a yearly salary. This proposition was accepted, and the Rev. Nathan Williams was ordained April 30, 1760. He continued the sole pastor of the church and society until January, 1813, a period of nearly fifty-three years, when the Rev. Ansel Nash was settled as his colleague. Doct. Williams continued to reside in Tolland until his decease, on the 15th of April, 1829, at the age of ninety-four years. He was born at Longmeadow, Mass., Nov. 8, 1735, was son of Rev. Stephen Williams, minister of that town, and grandson of Rev. John Williams, the celebrated minister of Deerfield.

The Rev. Nathan Williams, of Tolland, and Mary Hall, of Wallingford, were married October 20, 1760. The following were their children :

Nathan,	their son,	was born	Nov. 17, 1761, died in Savannah, Georgia, Dec. 16, 1784.
Eliakim Hall,	"	"	Jan. 16, 1764, died April 28, 1816.
William,	"	"	April 23, 1766.
Mary,	daughter,	"	April 19, 1768, married Doct. Wm. Grosvenor, Oct. 4, 1787.
Ruth,	"	"	Nov. 11, 1770, died October 2, 1788.
Abigail,	"	"	Aug. 14, 1773, died Feb. 2, 1774.
Isaac,	son	"	Sept. 24, 1776, died April 18, 1781.

Madam Mary Williams, relict of Doct. Williams, died March 9, 1833, aged ninety-five.

Only three of the children of Doct. Williams lived to be married. His son, Eliakim H. Williams, first married Mary Burt, daughter of David Burt, of Longmeadow, Mass., Jan. 18, 1792. She died January 22, 1793. He next married Damaris Cory, of Mansfield, February 1, 1797. She died September 20, 1801. He married for his third wife Aurelia Howard, of Tolland, January 9, 1803, with whom he lived until his death, April 28, 1816. By his last wife he had two sons and two daughters, viz.: Eliakim and Isaac;—and Emeline and Mary-Damaris-Aurelia. Mr. Eliakim H. Williams always resided in Tolland, and was town clerk at the time of his death. After his death his family removed to the State of New York, where they have since continued to reside.

William Williams, son of Doct. Nathan Williams, married Sarah Burt, of Longmeadow, Mass., September 4, 1793. They had seven sons, viz.: Nathan, William, David-Burt, Augustus-Davenport, Theodosicus-Dickerman, Charles-Albert, and Mortimer-Hall. Their daughters were Mary-Burt, and Sophia-Maria. This family lived in Tolland until the year 1833, when they removed into the western country.

Mary Williams, the daughter of Doct. Williams, married Doct. William Grosvenor, October 4, 1787. They lived in Tolland until Doct. Grosvenor's death, October 16, 1798. They had eight children, only three of whom survived infancy. The names of those were Mary-Williams, Ruth and Jacob. This family removed from Tolland after the decease of Doct. Grosvenor; and there has been no one of the lineal descendants of Doct. Williams, resident in the town since 1833.

The Rev. Doctor Williams holds a prominent place in the history of Tolland. He has done more than any other person to form the character of its inhabitants. He was their only minister for more than fifty years, and occupied a prominent and influential position for nearly seventy years of his life. In person he was about five feet nine inches in height; rather stout, with a body symmetrical and well proportioned. He was easy and graceful in his manners, social in his habits, and interesting and instructive in his conversation. He was punctilious in etiquette, careful in his personal appearance, precise and select in his language, and in every way a model gentleman of the old school. As a preacher he adhered to the tenets of the old divines, was strictly orthodox as the term was then understood, but was quite liberal for the age in which he lived. He was a good scholar, well educated, with a fair intellect, and good common-sense. His public performances were very creditable, and quite acceptable to his parishioners. Several of his sermons and other religious compositions were printed, and will compare favorably with similar productions of his associates. Several copies of them are now deposited in the library of the Connecticut Historical Society at Hartford. They were written and published as follows:

    In 1780. The Annual Election Sermon at Hartford.
        1788. On the Design and Importance of Christian Baptism.
        1792. On Christian Baptism and Discipline. Two editions.
        1793. Discourse on the Fourth of July, at Stafford.
        1793. Fast Day Sermon at Tolland. Order and Harmony in the Churches agreeable to God's Law.
        1794. Funeral Sermon at the Burial of Eliakim Hall.
        1795. Sermon at the Funeral of Rev. Nathan Strong, of Coventry.

Mrs. Mary Williams was a perfect model for a minister's wife. Intelligent without vanity; complacent without sycophancy; devotedly pious without any forbidding pretensions, she exercised a salutary influence without any apparent effort. She taught by example as well as by precept; and the duties of a wife and a mother were not neglected nor forgotten in the pursuit of those that belong to the visionary philanthropist, or the chimerical moralist. She attended to the duties of her own household, and cared for the wants of her dependants, feeling that her happiness was best promoted when she was contributing to the enjoyment of those around her. She was an economist, not for the purpose of acquiring wealth, but on account of the example to others. Doct. Williams possessed more of this world's goods, comparatively, than now ordinarily falls to the lot of country ministers, but it was never ostentatiously used. His house always exhibited comforts without extravagance, and great order and neatness without luxurious elegance. Mrs. Williams made it a matter of principle to live like her parishioners, although her means would have allowed her greater comforts. She was heard to say during the last years of her life, that her children when small, always went barefooted to meeting in summer, because some in the parish were unable to furnish their's with shoes at that season, so that no comparison could be instituted between her children and others in that respect. The principle that prompted this act, properly cultivated, would tend to restrain the practice now becoming a custom, of regarding the attire in which we are clad when in the sanctuary, as of more consequence than the services in which we are there engaged.

The Rev. ANSEL NASH was settled as the colleague of the Rev. Doctor Williams, in the month of January, 1813, and continued to be the active pastor of the church and society until the month of May, 1831, a period of a little more than eighteen years, when he was dismissed upon his own request, with the consent of a majority of the church and society.

Mr. Nash was born in Williamsburg, Hampshire County, Mass., on the 16th of January, 1788. He was the son of John Nash, of Williamsburg, and his wife, Martha Little, formerly of Granby, Conn. He graduated at Williams College in the year 1807, at the age of nineteen years. He pursued and finished his theological studies at Andover, Mass., and was licensed to preach in the year 1810. He came to Tolland in the latter part of the summer of 1812, received a call, and in January, 1813, was ordained as the colleague of Doctor Williams. His salary was six hundred dollars a year; one hundred of which, a few years later, he generously relinquished annually, in consideration of the pecuniary circumstances of the society. He was married to Eunice Jennings, of Windham, Conn., on the 24th of May, 1813, with whom he lived until his death. He left no children. After he was dismissed from Tolland he was settled in the ministry in Bloomfield, Hartford County, Conn., six years, when his relation with that people was dissolved, and he became the agent of the American Education Society awhile, and then the pastor of the first church in Rockville for about two years, when he was again dismissed. He was, at two different times, agent of the American Education Society, eight years, and supplied the pulpit in Colchester, Vermont, for about four years. While residing in Colchester, towards the close of his life, he became paralytic, and of unsound mind. In the vain hope that he could be benefited by the medical treatment and nursing at the insane hospital at Brattleborough, Vermont, he was sent to that institution in the summer of the year 1850, where, without receiving benefit, either in body or mind, from the change, he departed this life August 11, 1851, aged 63 years, 6 months, and 26 days.

Mr. Nash was a man of marked ability. To a mind naturally quick and active, was added the polish of a finished education; and aided by a memory that garnered the choicest treasures of both ancient and modern literature, he was prepared to acquit himself creditably on the theatre of life. His sermons were characterized rather for their logic than their rhetoric, and contained more of argument than imagination; still they were both attractive and instructive. He could not be said to be eloquent in their delivery, but was earnest, forcible and serious, and particularly successful in securing the attention of his hearers. In extemporary prayer he possessed peculiar gifts. He seemed to apprehend the secret desires of the most obscure worshiper present, and would present them at the mercy seat in language that raised the mind from earth to heaven, and imbued it with that fervency which makes prayer importunate and effectual.

Some of the productions of his pen have been published, among which are a Sermon on Christian Fellowship, printed in the National Preacher in the year 1831; a somewhat extended memoir of Mrs. Elizabeth Eldredge in the Panoplist in the year 1816; and other interesting articles in magazines and newspapers.

In social life, Mr. Nash was open, frank, and sometimes a little abrupt. He carefully noticed passing events, and was free to make them topics of general remark; and it was sometimes supposed these occupied too much of his time as a religious teacher. And yet he was never light nor trifling, and was always ready to defend the religion he professed, whenever and however assailed. His connection with secular matters, sometimes brought him in conflict with others engaged in similar pursuits, and was the cause of some uneasiness on the part of those who should have been his friends.

He strenuously maintained the right of exercising his own judgment in matters personal to himself, and yet he would not obstinately pursue a course of conduct offensive to any one, when he had reason to believe such conduct was not required by other demands than his own interest. He was forward in all efforts for public improvement in the town in which he lived—particularly those which had for their object the education of the masses. He took especial interest in the establishment of an academy in Tolland; and was for a long time chairman of the board of trustees. It may not be invidious to remark, that the academy ceased to exist about the time of Mr. Nash's leaving the town, and there has been no special effort since to revive it. He was a valuable member of society; an intelligent and interesting preacher; a worthy and revered pastor; and a most constant and sincere friend.

After the dismissal of Mr. Nash, the Rev. ABRAM MARSH became the pastor of the Congregational church and society in Tolland, which position he continues to occupy. He was installed on the 30th day of November, 1831. Mr. Marsh was born in Hartford, Vermont, June 15, 1802. He was educated at Dartmouth College, where he graduated in 1825; pursued his theological studies at Andover, Mass., and was licensed to preach in 1828. He supplied a church in Redding, Vermont, about two years, a portion of which time he was the principal of an academy at Thetford. He married Miss Rhoda Short, of Vermont, January 25, 1829, who died in Tolland, August 17, 1840, leaving two sons. Mr. Marsh married Miss Mary H. Cooley, of Norwich, Conn., his present wife, April 6, 1842.

As he is still the pastor of the church and society in Tolland, it is not proper for me to say more in this place; and may the day be distant when any pen will be employed in writing his biography.

From 1723 to the present time, a period of one hundred and thirty-eight years, the Congregational church and society have had but four settled ministers, and there has been but one year and two months vacation in the office during the whole time.

It has generally been supposed there were no differences of opinion on matters of religion among the inhabitants of Tolland before the year 1791, when the Methodists made their first location in this town. Although at the time of the settlement of Dr. Williams, and for thirty years thereafter, the people were of one fold and one shepherd, yet it is true that the inhabitants of Tolland, in common with the other towns in New England, were seriously affected by the preaching of Whitefield and his associates about the year 1745. The Rev. Wait Palmer, one of the preachers attached to that class of the followers of Mr. Whitefield that called themselves Separatists, labored in Tolland and its vicinity in the years 1750 and 1751, and received persons to his particular fellowship through the ordinance of baptism. This Mr. Palmer, and one Rev. Joshua Morse, administered the rite of ordination to one Shubael Stearns, Jr., of Tolland, of whom I shall speak more particularly in another place. Suffice it here to say, that Mr. Stearns was a most zealous leader of the Separatists, and held no fellowship with the church then under the charge of Rev. Mr. Steel. Mr. Stearns left the town, with his principal adherents, in the year 1754, after which there was no particular controversy by reason of this sect. Tradition informs us that the christian charity and sound judgment of Rev. Mr. Steel did very much to control the excited feeling of the people at this time, and continue their attachment to him, and to the church of which he was the pastor.

In the summer of 1791, the preachers of the Methodist denomination first visited the town of Tolland, and succeeded in establishing a Church. The names of their first preachers were Lee, Rayner and Hull. Their preaching was attended with very considerable success, and their followers became so numerous it was found necessary to have a house for public worship, and one was built in 1794. These preachers brought with them much of the zeal and many of the practices of the Separatists; and they attracted very great attention from the earnestness, and, what many supposed, the irregularities of their worship. This, doubtless, was the occasion of the fast-day sermon by the Rev. Dr. Williams, entitled, "Order and

Harmony in the Churches agreeable to God's Will," in which he speaks of the confusion and disorder of some worshiping assemblies as being contrary to the will of God. The organization of the Methodist church and society has continued with but occasional interruptions, in a regular supply of preachers according to the usages of that denomination, to the present time.

The Baptist church was organized in June, 1807. Their first minister was the Rev. Augustus Bolles, who was ordained their pastor in the year 1814. The services at his ordination were held in the Congregational meeting-house. He continued their minister three years. The next settled minister in this society was Rev. Levi Walker, Jr., who was ordained in June, 1833, and was succeeded by Rev. Sylvester Barrows in the year 1836, who continued their minister until the year 1841. Since the departure of Mr. Barrows, the following named gentlemen have supplied the Baptist church and society, viz.: Rev. John Hunt, one year; Rev. Jamas Squier, three years; Rev. George Mixter, two years; Rev. Thomas Holman, one year; Rev. Percival Matthewson, one year; Rev. Homer Sears, three years; Rev. Thomas Dowling, four years; Rev. Joseph A. Tillinghast, a little more than a year, until his death August 7, 1859; and Rev. C. L. Baker, who is now their minister. They have also been supplied occasionally by other persons.

MILITARY.

THE first record of any military organization in Tolland is under the date of October, 1722. The General Assembly then approved of Joseph Hatch as Lieutenant, and John Huntington as Ensign of the train-band in Tolland. The number in the "train-band" was probably then too small to make a captain necessary. The following return, copied from the archives in Hartford, for 1725, shows the election of the first captain of the train-band in this town.

"Major Wolcott, Esq. Pursuant to that order from yourself for the drawing of the first company in Tolland, to a choice for their commissioned officers for said company in Tolland; said company accordingly met on the 20th day of April and orderly chose Lieutenant Joseph Hatch, captain; Ensign John Huntington Lieutenant, and Joseph Pack Ensign.
EBENEZER NYE, Military Clerk."

Samuel Chapman was chosen in 1735, to succeed Joseph Hatch as captain of this company. By a return bearing date September 13, 1737, it appears that the roll of this company contained the names of eighty-seven rank and file. The militia were afterwards divided into two companies, called the north and south companies; the division of territory between the companies was a line nearly east and west through the town, passing across the south end of the Street; and west of the Street was represented by the road running west from the present residence of Mr. William West to Vernon line.

The extent of the participation of Tolland in the wars previous to that which commenced in 1755, can not now be ascertained. All that is known with certainty is, that Captain Samuel Chapman, Sen., commanded a company in the expedition to Louisburgh, in 1745, where he died the following January; and that Samuel Baker, son of Joseph Baker, in that, or a former war, died in captivity among the French and Indians.

In the year 1756, the colonies raised an army of seven thousand men for the purpose of aiding the mother country in an expedition against Crown point, and placed them under the command of Major-General Winslow. Azariah Wills, of Tolland, (brother of Solomon Wills, of whom I shall by and by have something to say,) enlisted under Capt. John Slap, in the service of the colonies, on the second day of April, 1756, and served until the 25th day of June following, when he was unfortunately taken prisoner, with others, by the French and Indians, between Albany and Hoosick, and carried to Canada. He remained a captive and endured great hardships until November, 1758, when he attempted to return with Col. Schuyler and Major Putnam, but while on his journey home he was taken sick and died on the eighteenth of November, 1758.

How many others from Tolland were in this expedition I am unable to say.

In August, 1757, there was an alarm that a powerful force of French and Indians was on the way to attack fort William Henry. Volunteers were called for, and Connecticut instantly poured forth several thousand. On the roll of Capt. Samuel Stoughton's company are found the names of the following men of Tolland.

Ens. Samuel Chapman, Nathan Harvey. Solomon Loomis, Simon Chapman,
Serg. Solomon Wills, David Hatch, Samuel Huntington, Francis West,
Daniel Baker, John Eaton, Jabez Bradley, Rufus West,
Elihu Johnson, Ichabod Hinckley, Samuel Barnard, Joseph Davis,
John Abbott, Jr , George Nye, Samuel Benton, Jr., John Stearns, Jr.,
Abner West, Timothy Delano, Samuel Aborn, Amos Ward.
Thacher Lathrop, William Benton, Jonathan Ladd, Jr., 28 in all.
Jacob Fellows,

But the French general, Montcalm, had prosecuted the siege with his usual vigor; and the fort was compelled to surrender before any of the volunteers could arrive. Those from Tolland went no further than Kinderhook, in the state of New York; and returned home, receiving pay for only fifteen day's service. Pay was allowed for four horses from Tolland to Kinderhook, £2, 3s., 9d.; for nineteen from Tolland to Litchfield, £4, 18s., 11d.; and for two to bring them back from Litchfield, 14s., 5d.

For the campaign of 1758, Connecticut agreed to furnish five thousand men; and a company was formed in Tolland and its vicinity, of which Samuel Chapman, of Tolland, was captain. The following is a copy of the roll of his company.

*Capt. Sam. Chapman, *Jonathan Boroughs, William Hoskins, *Lemuel Hatch,
1st Lieut. Titus Olcott, *Abner West, Daniel Pratt, *Jabez Bradley,
2d Lieut. George Cooley, *Hope Lathrop, Abraham Whipple, *Joseph Luce,
*Ensign Solomon Wills, Timothy Ladd, John Atchison, Abijah Markham,
Serg. Samuel Benton, Jacob Newell, Oliver Chapin, Thomas Burns,
* "   Jonathan Birge, John Isham, Hezekiah Spencer, Hezekiah Wells,
   "   Abner Webb, *Lathrop Shurtliff, John Fuller, Jacob Hills,
* "   James Steel, clerk, John Gray, Joseph Buell, Simeon Webster,
Corp. Samuel Hall, *Joseph Davis, Alexander Gowdy, *Solomon Loomis,
   "   Jonathan Bill, Hezekiah Waters, Thomas Buck, Joseph Tilden,
   "   Asa Wood, Isaac Hills, Samuel Bartlett, . Joel Daniels,
   "   Nath'n Boardman,,Joshua Hutchins, Luke Parsons, Samuel Carver,
Drum'er, Henry Bowen, Jonathan Dart, Thomas Waters, John Gordon,
   "   Charles King, Joseph Spencer, James Kibbee, Samuel Darling,
Fifer, Joseph Conant. Beriah Bronson, James Pease, Joshua Bill,
   Privates. Hezekiah King, Nathaniel Brace, Joseph Pike,
*William Benton, Samuel Hutchinson, Jacob Ward, Nathan Tiffany,
*Moses West, Joseph Tucker, Abner Pease, Joshua Allen,
*John Lathrop, Jonathan Buckland, John Ford, Josiah Fields,
*Joseph Eaton, Samuel Blackmore, Jonathan Phelps, *Nathaniel Warren,
Daniel Brewster, Jonathan Wright, William Russell, Joseph Crocker.
Joseph Heath, Lemuel Jones, *Nathan Harvey,
Benjamin Burdon, David Talcott, Jonathan Bliss, Officers and music'ns, 15
Joseph Whitcomb, Moses Thrall, *Shubael Dimick, Privates, . . 80
*John Barnard, Brinton Payne, Benjamin Shepherd, Total, . . 95

Twenty-one of the above, viz.: those marked *, are recognized as belonging in Tolland, and probably there were others. Most of the remainder would be recognized by their names as having gone from the towns of Somers, Mansfield, Willington, Bolton, Coventry, and East Windsor.

In the year 1762, the King of England made a requisition upon the colonies for troops to join in the expedition against the island of Cuba; and a company was raised in the eastern part of the State, of which Col. Israel Putnam was, by one of the then formalities of the service, nominally captain, but really under the command of its first lieutenant, Solomon Wills, of Tolland. This company went to the island of Cuba, and was present at the siege and capture of Havana, but was not in any serious engagement. When a boy, I was informed by a man whose name is on the roll, that after the principal fort had been undermined and blown up, so that a column of British regulars carried it by assault, this company had the sad duty to perform of clearing the fort and burying the dead. The destruction of life was very great; the dead were represented as lying in winrows. The pools of blood were so deep in some places in the fort that, as my informant said, he was compelled to step over his shoes in human gore while removing the dead. Although this company was not under fire during the whole of this campaign, the mortality of its members was unparalleled. Of the ninety-eight persons of which the company was composed and who actually reached the Island, only twenty-two ever returned to their native land. Of the twenty-seven enlisted from Tolland and its vicinity, only four escaped the arrow of the fell destroyer. The names of two of these four persons were Solomon Wills and Edward Hatch. John Barnard, John Burrows, Constant Crandall, William Eaton, Aaron Eaton, Leonard Grover, Judah Hatch, Noah Stimson, Ezra Waldo and Oliver Yeomans, of Tolland, are known to have died on the Island of Cuba. There were no deaths in the company before the month of August. As returned on the roll, the deaths were, in August, fifteen; in September, eighteen; in October, eighteen; in November, eighteen; and in December, seven.

THE EARLY HISTORY OF TOLLAND. 47

Total, seventy-six. The survivors were paid off December 11, 1762. The average term of service was about thirty-five weeks. The following is the pay-roll of this company. Those marked † died during the campaign.

Israel Putnam, Capt.,
*Solo. Wills, 1st Lieut,
Alex. Chalker, 2d "
†Isaac Dana, Ensign,
†Moses Earl, Sergeant,
Samuel Hyde, "
Samuel Cotton,
   or "
   Colton,
†Nath'l Wheeler, "
*†Const. Crandal, "
†Jos. Truesdale, Corp'l,
Silas Harris, "
†Thomas Brewer, "
†Joshua Reed, "
   Privates.
†John Abby,
†Nathan Allen,
†Squire Allen,
†Henry Bradley,
Samuel Bliss,
†Jonathan Bliss,
†Rinaldo Burdon,
*†John Barnard,
*†John Burrows,
†Stephen Brace,

†Daniel Brace,
James Belbon,
†Daniel Brewer,
†William Case,
†John Croswell,
†Edmund Cadwell,
†John Curtis,
†Joseph Croswell,
†John Cross,
†Ebenezer Dana,
†Reuben Downing,
John Dollaby,
†Elijah Durphy,
†Cornelius Downing,
†Joel Daniels,
*†William Eaton,
†Joseph Edgerton,
*†Aaron Eaton,
Timothy Evans,
†William Ellis,
†Abraham Forbes,
†David Fuller,
*†Leonard Grover,
†Stephen Goff,
†Ezekiel Guernsey,

*†Judah Hatch,
*Edward Hatch,
†Joseph Hayward,
†Asahel Hollister,
†Robert Hollister,
†Jacob Hollister,
John Hero,
†Nathaniel Holt,
†Ebenezer Holmes,
†Jonathan Johnston,
†William Kimball,
Thomas Knapping,
†Benj. Langworthy,
†Benjamin Loveman,
†John Negus,
†Richard Orms,
†Abraham Porter,
†Nathaniel Redington,
†John Read,
Ackley Riley,
†John Ripponer,
†Thomas Rose,
†Matthew Raymond,
†Daniel Roberts,
*†Noah Stimson,
†Amos Shurtliff,

†Simon Strickland,
†Samuel Stiles,
†Israel Saunders,
†Amos Staples,
†Isaac Staples,
Nathaniel Stone,
†Jonathan Sampson,
†Jedediah Sanger,
†Samuel Smith,
John Stark,
Benjamin Shaw,
Charles Shorvel,
†Samuel Williams,
†Joseph Whitcomb,
John Way,
†Ebenezer Wheeler,
*†Ezra Waldo,
*†Oliver Yeomans,
†Christopher Lucas,
†Caleb Shepard,
†Ebenezer Shaw.

Taken by the Sheriff.
Joseph Bisbee,
Samuel Stanley.

The following names are marked, Deserted: Sanuel Blackman, Gideon Burnham, John Brown, Joel Brooks, Noadiah Bronson, John Part, Ephraim Foot, Lot Loveland, Joseph Prout, Asahel Hollister, John Adams.

The war of the Revolution commenced in 1775, and was most vigorously supported by the people of Tolland County, particularly by the town of Tolland. Their experience in the war of 1755, known as the French war, had made 'them acquainted with the trials and hardships of military life, and prepared them for the duties of the camp in the approaching struggle with the mother country. Not only did the town furnish its full quota of men and officers for the field, but it was also forward in contributing to the relief of those who suffered for advocating the principles that led to our national independence. The first town meeting touching the difficulties between the colonies and England was held on the fifth day of September, 1774. Ichabod Griggs was chosen moderator. The following is a copy of the record of that meeting:

"Voted, That Messrs. Samuel Cobb, Solomon Wills, and Eleazar Steel be the delegates to attend the county meeting at Hartford on the 15th instant.

Voted, That Samuel Cobb Esq., Capt. Solomon Wills, Capt. Elijah Chapman and Ensign Eleazer Steel be a committee of correspondence for this town, to receive and answer letters from the committees of correspondence in the several towns of this and the other colonies relative to the public controversy.

Voted, That Messrs. Stephen Day, James Chamberlin, Hope Lathrop, Joseph West and Simon Chapman, be a committee to receive and transmit to the towns of Boston and Charlestown, such charitable donations as shall be subscribed for the use of the poor and necessitous inhabitants of those towns.

Voted, That the selectmen be empowered and directed by the town to procure powder and other ammunition fully to supply the town stock, in proportion as the law directs at the expense of the town.

Voted, That a copy of these resolves unanimously agreed to, be transmitted to the press; and the town-clerk be directed to forward them."

The appointment of the committee to receive charitable donations for the use of the poor and necessitous of the towns of Boston and Charlestown, was not an unmeaning formality, but was prompted by that generous sincerity with which the people of that age were actuated. The following copy of a letter dated Boston, October 24, 1774, about six weeks after this appointment, will show the object the town had in view, and the efficiency with which the committee discharged its duties.

"Gentlemen, This is to acknowledge the receipt of your kind and generous donation of ninety-five sheep by the hand of our worthy friend Mr. Hope Lathrop which shall be applied to the relief of our poor sufferers by means of the cruel and oppressive port bill,—according to the intentions of the generous donors. We are still struggling under the heavy load of tyranny. Our troubles are exceedingly great, but the kindness and benevolence of our friends in Tolland, as well as other places, greatly refreshes and raises our spirits. You may depend upon it, that by divine help and blessing, Boston will suffer every thing with patience and firmness that a cruel and arbitrary administration can inflict upon us, even to the loss of fortune and life, rather than submit in any one instance to the power of tyranny. We trust we have a righteous cause, and that the Supreme Ruler of the Universe will in his own time and way, arise and scatter the dark clouds that at present hang over us. We submit to him and ask your prayers at the throne of grace for us. The sincere thanks of this committee in behalf of this greatly distressed and injured town are hereby presented to our worthy friends in Tolland, for their kind assistance in this our day of trial. We are with great esteem, gentlemen, your friends and fellow countrymen.

HENRY HILL, per order of the committee of Donations."

Nor did the liberality of the town cease on the commencement of hostilities, nor was it confined to direct drafts upon its own treasury for the support of the soldiers of the war and their families. The following document, copied from the original in the office of the town clerk, is evidence that the town was ever ready to do its part in relieving sufferers under all circumstances.

"Tolland, Dec. 21, 1781. Rec'd of the Selectmen of the town of Tolland in hard money £3.14.6; ($12.42;) States money with the Interest—£3.12.1, ($12.01;) as a donation from said town for the relief of the suffering inhabitants of New London and Groton, agreeable to a late brief issued by his Hon. the Governor.

STEPHEN STEEL, Town Treas'r."

When it is remembered that the massacre at Fort Griswold, in the town of Groton, and the burning of New London took place on the 6th day of September, 1781, we can not entertain any doubt as to the cause of the sufferings which this donation, amounting to twenty-four dollars, forty-five cents, was intended to relieve.

Under date of December 19, 1774, the town " voted that the selectmen do immediately double the town stock of ammunition at the town expense." On the same day, they " voted that Samuel Cobb Esq., Capt. Elijah Chapman, Ensign Eleazar Steel, Capt. Solomon Wills and Samuel Chapman Esq., shall be a committee of observation for effectual putting in execution the doings of the continental Congress, expressed in the ninth article of the association and directed in the eleventh article of said association."

All these proceedings were preliminary to the commencement of hostilities, which event occurred at Lexington, Mass., April 19, 1775. When the news of this transaction reached

Tolland, a company of men was immediately formed from this and several neighboring towns, which, under the command of Capt. Solomon Wills, served in Col. Spencer's regiment at Roxbury, near Boston, from May 1, to December 1, 1775, a period of eight months. The following is a copy of the roll of this company, kept by Comfort Carpenter, its orderly sergeant, and filed by him in the Pension Office as evidence of his service in the war of the revolution, with his application for a pension, under the act of June 7, 1832.

*Solomon Wills, Capt.,
Jona. Parker, 1st Lieut.
Samuel Felt, 2d "
Noah Chapin, Ensign,
*Com. Carpenter, Serg.,
Abel Parker, "
Jacob Orcutt, "
Noah Cooley, "
*Heman Baker, Jr. "
Jonah Brown, "
*Elij'h Chapman, Corp.
Asa Fenton, "
Matthew Buel. "
*Luke Washburn, "
*Samuel Steel, "
*Jas. Steel, Jr., Drum'r
*Joel Stinson, Fifer,
Elias Newton, "
    Privates.
Amasa Allen,
*John Abbott,
Moses Amadon,
Jude Brown,
Jacob Brown,
Alexander Brown,

Amasa Buck,
Elijah Bradley,
*Jonathan Burrough,
Josiah Bradley,
*Josiah Benton,
*Jonathan Benton,
*Azariah Benton,
Asa Baldwin,
Jacob Brown, 2d,
Nathan Carpenter,
Eliphalet Cushman,
*Richmond Crandal,
*John Carlton,
*David Carlton,
*Richard Carlton,
*Ebenezer Cook,
John Charter,
Charles Day,
*Edward Dimock,
William Elmer,
Adonijah Fenton,
John Furman,
*Isaac Fellows,
Christopher Frantz,
Simeon Griswold,

*Samuel Benton,
*Ebenezer Grant,
*John Huntington,
*David Hinckley,
Ezra Holmes,
*Abner Hatch,
*Dan Hatch,
Levi Hamlin,
Nathan Jennings,
Samuel Johnson,
Caleb Johnson,
Daniel Johnson,
Daniel Kibbee,
James Kibbee,
Bildad Kibbee,
John Lewis,
Edward Lawrence,
Andrew Miner,
Caleb Orcutt,
John Orcutt,
Peter Pinney,
Abner Pease,
*Rufus Price,
Moses Pelton,
Joshua Parks,

*Tyrus Preston,
*Ammi Paulk,
Nathan Root,
Joseph Root,
Jeremiah Rider,
Daniel Rice,
Stephen Rice,
John Scripter,
*Perez Steel,
John Shurtliff,
Elisha Stebbins,
Isaiah Sparks,
Simeon Stimson,
Jeremiah Sparks,
*Nehemiah Sabin,
Joseph Sexton,
Elijah Sexton,
*Henry Stevens,
Stephen Taylor,
Justus Thompson,
Samuel Wright,
*Jabez West,
*Elijah Washburn,
Noah Whipple.

Those who have been ascertained with certainty to have gone from Tolland are marked *, but it is known there were more. The number on the roll are—officers and musicians, eighteen; privates, eighty. Total, ninety-eight. The names indicate that the men were from Tolland, Somers, Stafford, Willington, and Coventry. Arrangements for enlisting were made in Tolland and men engaged on the day the news of the battle of Lexington reached the place. It is known that other persons from Tolland were at Roxbury, but were either temporary substitutes, or in other companies; among them were Joshua Griggs and Solomon Eaton. Thirty-four are known as belonging in Tolland, which town was ascertained the previous year to contain twelve hundred and forty-seven white, and fifteen black inhabitants. The last survivor of the Tolland men on the roll was Capt. Ammi Paulk, who died in 1843. Moses Pelton was from Somers, and the next year when the Americans retreated from New York, he was killed by a cannon ball from the British shipping.

On the first day of April, 1777, the town voted to furnish the families of men who would enlist into the continental service, with provisions and other necessaries, and appointed Capt. James Chamberlin, Lieut. Stephen Day, and Ensign Eleazar Steel, a committee for that purpose. The town also voted to present to each soldier that should so enlist, a bounty of ten pounds in money, (thirty-three dollars and thirty-three cents;) one-half to be paid at the end of one year from April 1, 1777, and the other half at the end of the second year: "Provided the Honorable Assembly shall not raise money for the purpose; but if the Assembly shall add to the soldiers bounty or wages, the sum of ten pounds, then the town is quit and free from this vote and obligation aforesaid; and if the assembly shall add any part of said sum of ten pounds to the soldiers [bounty or pay,] as aforesaid, then it is to be understood to be in part pay of said sum of ten pounds to be given as aforesaid." It appears by the other proceedings that these enlistments were to be for three years or during the war.

From the record of the Committee of Payables, under date of July 16, 1787, I find the vote of April, 1777, was responded to, and the bounty of ten pounds therein named, was paid to the following persons, viz.:

William Johnson,	William Sowle,	Joseph Cogswell.	Andrew Miner,
Solomon Eaton,	Simon Stimson,	Elijah Haskell,	Tyrus Preston,
Ebenezer Brown,	Joseph Sparks,	Richard Carlton.	Nehemiah Sabin,
Isaac Squier,	Jonathan Luce,	Jacob Haskell,	Andrew Peterson,
John P. Burrows,	Clement Miner,	Elijah Benton,	Elihu Johnson,
Abel Craudall,	Brisley Harris,	George Hubbard,	Ebenezer Stebbins.
Ammi Paulk,	William Huntington,	Elias Newton,	

Twenty-seven in all, who received £270. Solomon Eaton, the last known survivor, died in Tolland in September, 1843. The above-named men belonged to Capt. Ichabod Hinckley's company, and formed a part of the second Connecticut Regiment. There is a roll of Capt. Hinckley's company still extant, from which the following names are copied. Those marked *, were from Tolland:

*Capt. I. Hinckley,	Corp. Nehemiah Sabin,	*Martin Davis,	*Abel Crandal,
*Lieut. E. Chapman,	*Jonathan Luce,	*William Huntington,	*John P. Burroughs,
*Lieut. Rufus Price,	*Elihu Johnson,	*William Johnson,	*William Sowle,
*Dr. Jeremiah West,	*Tyrus Preston,	*Solomon Eaton,	*Shubael Dimick,
Serj. Eben'r Stebbins,	*Andrew Peterson,	Ebenezer Brown,	*Edy Hatch,
*Serj. Ammi Paulk,	*Elias Newton,	Isaac Squier,	*Simon Stimson,

*Jonathan Delano,   John Crandall,   Joseph Sparks,   David Pierce,
*Clement Miner,   *George Hubbard. Amos Harris,   Roswell Miner.
*Jacob Haskell,   *Elijah Benton,   *Richard Carlton,

On the 23d of September, 1777, the town "voted to comply with the resolve of the Governor and Council of this State, in providing articles of clothing for the soldiers in the continental army belonging to the town." The following persons were appointed a committee for that purpose :

Samuel Cobb, Esq.,   Hope Lathrop,   Daniel Edgerton,   Elijah Yeomans,
Capt. E. Chapman,sen., Adoniram Grant,   Eleazar Hammond, Jr., Lieut. David Jewett,
 " Jas. Chamberlin,   Samuel Nye,   Shubael Dimick,   Elnathan Strong,
 " Stephen Steel,   Rufus Price,   Titus Baker,   Samuel Ladd,
 " Stephen Day,   Elias Holbrook,   Eleazar Steel.   Jonathan Ladd.
 " Stephen Stimson,   John Palmer,   George Nye,   29 in all.
Col. Solomon Wills,   Jabez Bradley,   Azariah Post,
Eleazar Kingsbury,   Amos James,   John Steel,

December 8, 1777. Aaron Woodward, John Tyler, John Steel, and Joseph West, were chosen a committee to provide for the families of non-commissioned officers and soldiers belonging to the continental army from Tolland, for the year ensuing.

January 1, 1778. Under this date I find the following vote : " Voted, that we accept and approve the articles of confederation drawn up by the Congress of the United States ; and do view them as a well-formed plan of confederation and perpetual union. Voted nem. con."

In making provision for the soldiers of the revolution, it became necessary to have a deposit for military stores, and on the 28th day of December, 1778, Elias Holbrook was appointed to take care of the military stores belonging to the town.

Hope Lathrop and Benoni Shepard were on the 28th day of June, 1779, appointed a committee " to provide clothing for the officers and soldiers in the continental army belonging in Tolland ; " and the selectmen were empowered " to settle with the committee appointed to provide such clothing and pay them therefor."

The war had now continued about five years, and the issue was still doubtful. The credit of the government had depreciated, and the circulating medium of the country had become nearly worthless. The army began to complain as well for the non-payment of its wages as the worthlessness of the currency in which it was paid. It was impossible to find men willing to leave their families for the continental service, without further guarantees that their services should be fairly compensated. The town of Tolland was required to furnish sixteen men for the continental army for the year 1780, besides its quota of cavalry. In order to obtain this number by voluntary enlistment, the town, on the 26th day of June, 1780, voted that the wages of forty shillings per month should be kept good, and made up to each effective man belonging to the town who should enlist to serve until the last day of the then next December in the Connecticut line of the continental army; in wheat at four shillings per bushel; rye at three shillings per bushel, and Indian corn at two shillings per bushel. And as a further encouragement the town voted to pay each man that should so enlist, the sum of thirty shillings, lawful money, on the first day of January then next. By the same vote they extended the benefit of the same allowance to such effective men as should enlist into the cavalry to serve in the continental army the same time. On the fifth day of July, 1780, they offered the same benefit to such as should voluntarily enlist for three months, except the bounty, which was fifteen shillings instead of thirty—and to be paid January 1, 1781. The following persons received the bounty of thirty shillings in silver, voted July 5, 1780, to wit: Samuel Steel, Lot Burgess, Aaron Delano, Sylvanus Gage, Eleazar Hatch, William Johnson, Ezra Rawdon, Andrew Steel, Zadock Benton, Samuel Chase, Hezekiah Huntington, Samuel Reed, Manoah Crowell, Clement Miner, Luther Delano, and Solomon Loomis. They were in the second Connecticut Regiment, and served in Capt. Ichabod Hinckley's company, except Samuel Steel and Luther Delano, who died before the term of service expired. Samuel Reed, who died in Tolland in July, 1851, at the age of ninety-one, was the last survivor of the above, and *the last* revolutionary soldier in Tolland.

The same year, 1780, Benjamin Kimball, Charles Stearns, Ichabod West, Titus Hammond, Jacob Benton, and Joel Crandal, (six in all,) performed a tour of duty of three months. Jacob Benton died in Tolland in June, 1843.

These several obligations made it necessary for the town to provide means to discharge them, and many expedients were resorted to, to sustain the plighted faith of the town. Taxes payable in provisions as well as money, were laid; and such taxes as would frighten the tax payers of modern times. The Assembly had voted a tax of sixpence on the pound, payable in provisions, but it would seem that this tax was not fully paid, or was insufficient for the purpose. The town, therefore, on the 13th day of November, 1780 :

"Voted to raise a rate of one shilling on the list given in last year, for the purpose of raising the town's quota of provisions for the army and navy, *to be paid in silver or gold,* by the 15th of January next. Provided the inhabitants of this town or any of them, should not pay sixpence on the pound as the law directs in provisions. But in case they or as many of them as shall pay and deliver in provisions said sixpence on the pound to the receivers of provisions in this town according to law at the stated price and produce receipt therefor from said receivers, shall be discharged from said tax or vote."

Eleazar Steel and Medad Hart were appointed receivers of provisions for the town.

It became difficult to obtain a sufficient number of persons to make up the quota of the town in the continental army by voluntary enlistment, so many of its men being already enlisted either for a long stated term or during the war. Notwithstanding the encouragement the town had from time to time given, they were compelled to resort to such compulsory measures as should enable them to meet the demand. One mode adopted was, to divide the inhabitants of the town into classes and require each class to furnish one man. At the town meeting held on the 13th day of November, 1780, Col. Solomon Wills, Eleazar Kingsbury, Stephen Stimson, Benoni Shepard, Elijah Chapman, Hope Lathrop, and Miner Hilliard, were appointed a committee to class the inhabitants of the town for the purpose of furnishing its quota for the continental army. January 10, 1781, Ashbel Chapman and Jabez West were appointed a committee to provide clothing for the soldiers. February 9, 1781, Col. Solomon Wills,' Hope Lathrop, Capt. Elijah Chapman, Capt. Benjamin Norris, and Samuel Ladd, were chosen a committee to enlist five men to join a regiment and go to Horseneck for one year's service. They were empowered to divide the town into five classes, provided they could not hire the men by the 19th of the month. It appears that the committee could not hire them within the time specified, and they made a report of their classification of the town to an adjourned meeting held on the twenty-first of the same month, which was accepted and established. The town also voted to pay to each of the five classes, twelve pounds in silver money, ($40.00,) immediately upon their procuring a man for the class to enlist into the State service for one year. The following persons were hired by the classes, and received the bounty of twelve pounds each, promised in the vote:

William Barnard,   John Haskell,   Noah Johnson,   Walter Holmes,
Abner Squier.

On the 25th day of February, 1792, the town voted to "raise five men for the service at Horseneck, by a rate on the town at large." Simon Chapman, Col. Solomon Wills, John Steel, Medad Hunt, and Capt. Ichabod Hinckley, were appointed a committee to hire the men. The selectmen were empowered and directed to pay this committee the sums of money that they were "obliged to give the recruit as bounty for encouraging [engaging] in the service out of the town tax granted in December previous." In this instance, instead of determining the bounty themselves, the town left it to the discretion of this committee. There was some difference of opinion in regard to the number of men Tolland ought to furnish for the continental service; and at the meeting last-mentioned, the town appointed Col. Solomon Wills a committee to wait on the county committee and adjust the matter, as well as that relating to the year's men at Horseneck. Under the vote of February 25, 1782, as above, the following persons were engaged to serve one year at Horseneck, and each received twelve pounds bounty, viz.: William Barnard, John Haskell, Charles De Wolf, Abner Johnson, and Edy Hatch.

In 1782, the inhabitants of the town were divided into twenty-one classes, and procured for the continental army the twenty-one men whose names follow: Abel Stimson, Solomon Eaton, Ichabod West, Ichabod Case, James Covil, Samuel Parks and Allen Carpenter, Joshua Simons, John Haskell, Moses Coy, Samuel Dimock and Oliver Scott, Eliphalet Kilbourn, William Coltrain, Eleazar Hatch, Jonathan Creasy, John Dimick, Caleb Thomas, Sylvanus Gage, Reuben Robinson, Joel Barnard and William Eldredge.

·The following document, copied from the original in the town clerk's office, is valuable for locating the persons therein named:

" Received of Colonel Samuel Chapman, thirty-nine able-bodied men, viz.: Eliab Allen, Thomas Buck, Jr., Lot Burgess, Zadoc Benton, William Barnard, Samuel Billings, Jedediah Cady, Abner Cady, Samuel Chase, Samuel Davis, Job Davis, Eliab Edson, Israel Furman, Timothy Green, Ede Hatch, Walter Holmes, Timothy Herington, Philemon Holt, Hezekiah Huntington, William Johnson, Joseph Lamb, Jasper Marsh, Henry McNeil, Clement Miner, Benjamin Jones Orcutt, Solomon Parsons, Jeremiah Philips, Samuel Philips, Edy Pratt, Charles Pease, Samuel Reed, Sanford Richardson, Ezra Rawdon, Joshua Simons, Samuel Taylor, Brodwell Watkins, John West, Asa Wood, to answer as part of the quota to be furnished by his Regiment to serve in the continental army. JOHN P. WYLLIS, Capt.,
Hartford, July 6, 1780. Continental Army."

There is a memorandum on the back of this paper, as follows:

TOLLAND.	SOMERS.	STAFFORD.
Edy Hatch,	Samuel Davis,	Charles Wood,
Samuel Reed,	Edy Pratt,	William Washburn,
William Barnard,	Job Davis,	Asa Allen.
Joshua Simons,	Thomas Buck, jr.,	
William Johnson,	Solomon Parsons,	
Luther Delano,	Jeremiah Phillips,	
Samuel Chase,	Israel Inman,	
Ezra Rawdon,	Asa Wood,	
Hezekiah Huntington,	Charles Pease,	
Abner Johnson,	Ben. Jones Orcutt,	
Lot Burgess,	Sanford Richardson,	
Walter Holmes,	John Archer,	
Clemet Miner,	Samuel Billings. (13.)	
Samuel Park,		
Zadoc Benton,		
Moses Delano. (16.)		

The following are the names of the officers, citizens of Tolland, who served in the wars previous to the war of the revolution, viz.:

Samuel Chapman, Sen., was a captain in the war of 1745.

Samuel Chapman, Jr., was a captain in the war of 1755.

Samuel Huntington was an ensign in the war of 1755.

Solomon Wills was an ensign in the war of 1755; and Lieutenant commanding a company in the expedition to Cuba, 1762.

Probably there were several others who can not be now identified.

The following named persons, citizens of Tolland, were officers in the army of the Revolution, viz.:

Samuel Chapman, Colonel of the twenty-second Regiment of militia, from May, 1775, to May, 1792. His regiment was at New York in the year 1776, and performed a tour of duty of two months. He was in the service at other times.

Solomon Wills was Colonel during several tours of duty, either of State or Continental troops.

Ichabod Hinckley was a captain in the continental line.

Elijah Chapman (afterwards sheriff) was a captain in the continental line; and a part of the time in Lafayette's light infantry.

James Chamberlin was a captain of cavalry two campaigns.

Amos Fellows commanded one of the Tolland companies at New York.

Lieut. Lathrop, of the militia, was in active service.

Ichabod Griggs, ensign of the Tolland militia, campaign at New York.

Joshua Griggs, adjutant. His services were principally at Roxbury, New York and Saratoga.

There were two companies of militia in Tolland in 1776, both of which were in Col. Samuel Chapman's regiment at New York. But at this time only the names of the officers above given can be ascertained.

The following are the names of the persons, citizens of Tolland, who died in the various wars prior to the close of the revolutionary war in 1783:

Samuel Chapman, Sen., Captain, died at Louisburgh, January, 1746.

Samuel Baker died in captivity among the French and Indians.

Azariah Wills died during his return from captivity, November, 1758, aged 25.

William Benton died at Oswego in 1760, aged 35.

Samuel Huntington, Ensign, died at Lake Oneida, August 18, 1760, aged 32.

Constant Crandall died at Havana, Cuba, August 27, 1762.
Noah Stimson,   do. Sept. 13, 1762, Æ 20.
Jonathan Burroughs,   do.   "   7,   "
Wm. Eaton, son of William,   do. Oct. 18,   "   Æ 30.
John Barnard, son of Dr. Thos.,   do.   "
John Burrows,   do.   "
Aaron Eaton,   do.   "
Judah Hatch, son of Ichabod,   do.   "   Æ 42.
Oliver Yeomans,   do.   "
Ezra Waldo,   do.   "
Leonard Grover,   do.   "

Reuben Heath, son of Isaac Heath, died at Roxbury, Mass., September, 1775, aged 20.

A Mr. Scott, of Tolland, died at New York in 1776, before the city was evacuated.

Ichabod Griggs, Ensign, died at New Rochelle, N. Y., September 30, 1776.

Moses Barnard, son of Dr. Thomas, died at New Rochelle, October 15, 1776.

Azariah Benton, son of Daniel, died in a prison ship near New York, December 29, 1776, aged 22.

Amos Fellows, Captain, died in captivity in New York, February 17, 1777.

William Hatch, son of Joseph, Jr., died at Chatham, New Jersey, March 26, 1777, aged 30.

John Lathrop, son of John, was killed by a sabre cut at Horseneck, December 10, 1780, aged 18.

Heman Baker, Jr., died of small pox, at East Hartford, on his way from captivity.

Samuel Steel died in 1780.

Luther Delano died in 1780.

Aaron Steel, son of James, died in New Jersey.

Amos Cobb, son of Samuel Cobb, M. D., was killed at the White Plains.

The above are collected from the records. It is known there were many others, particularly at New York in 1776, but their names can not be ascertained.

It is impossible to estimate with accuracy the number of men belonging in Tolland who served in the army of the revolution. The quota usually assigned to it was from sixteen to twenty-one. I understand this did not include those who served in the cavalry. There can be no doubt that the town constantly had no less than twenty-five men in the field, besides those who served in what were called the *short levies,* and when the entire military force of the town went on some alarm or emergency. Nearly twenty can be enumerated as having gone from the present limits of the fifth school district; and probably more than one hundred and fifty persons, residents of Tolland, comprising nearly every man of suitable age and strength, participated in that struggle by marching against the enemy. Several persons were in the field during almost the entire war, among whom Capt. (afterwards Gen.) Elijah Chapman, Jonathan Luce, Isaac Fellows, Solomon Eaton, and Elihu Johnson are remembered. Several times almost the entire active male population was absent in the army, and ordinary work upon the farms was done by female hands. Elderly ladies sometimes spoke of their share of it in earlier life, as if it was among their most interesting recollections. I have heard a venerable lady, daughter of one of the revolutionary officers of Tolland, relate that she, assisted by her younger sisters, frequently yoked the oxen, and harvested the autumnal crops with their own hands. These necessary out of door duties had not the effect of producing masculine habits in those who engaged in them, or in making them less useful and agreeable in their proper sphere. In the instance above alluded to, they detracted nothing from the eminent social refinement and feminine graces of the individuals spoken of.

Although Tolland furnished its full proportion of men in the revolutionary contest, and although so many of them perished in the service, yet I have not been able to ascertain either by record or traditionary evidence, that any were slain in battle, except Amos Cobb and John Lathrop, before referred to. The record of John Lathrop's death, in the town-clerk's office, is as follows: "John, the son of John Lathrop, and Lucy his wife, departed this life December the 10th day,

1780, by the sword of the enemy at Horseneck." He was under eighteen years of age, and was struck dead by a blow on the head with a sabre, by a dragoon. Col. Solo. Wills, to whose wife Mr. Lathrop was nephew, assisted in wrapping him in his blanket and laying him in the grave of the soldier.

Nor is there now any evidence that any Tolland soldier received any dangerous wound, or so severe an one as to occasion his dimissal from the service.

Several kinds of domestic manufacture were attempted in Tolland in the revolution. Linen cloth was then made in families from flax, and exclusively used for summer clothing. There was a family named Morey who lived at the south end of the village street, near the residence of the late Jeremiah Parish, Esq., who used to print this home-made linen for ladies' dresses. The cloth being first whitened, was then impressed with figures engraved on a thin board very similar in size to the hand-cards used in those days—the impression being entirely done by hand. The only color distinctly recollected was a dark brown. It is much to be regretted that none of this cloth or the stamps have been preserved as most interesting revolutionary relics.

There was also an attempt to manufacture molasses from green corn-stalks, ground in a common cider mill, and pressed like pomace of apples. The particular mill used for this purpose stood just back of the site on which was afterward built the house in which Col. Elijah Smith kept a tavern for half a century.

In the south-west part of the town resided Mr. Titus Baker, a blacksmith, and his brother, Mr. Joseph Baker, who possessed great natural ingenuity in the mechanical arts. In the scarcity of muskets, they contrived to manufacture a number, (it is not known how many,) which, though clumsy and heavy, were reputed to be serviceable weapons. The makers estimated that the labor bestowed on one of them amounted to the time of one man a fortnight.

During the war there were several instances in which British prisoners were sent to Tolland for support and safe keeping. In the year 1781, when the progress of the war in the

South rendered it necessary to remove the army of Burgoyne from Virginia, where they were sent for cantonment after their surrender, many of them were removed into Connecticut. Companies of Hessians were quartered on the premises of Col. Wills, lately the property of Jonas Green; also at the house now occupied by Theodore Chapin. At one time, two Hessian officers had a dispute and arranged for a duel, which was only prevented by the assurance that in case of the death of either, our laws would in due season, without fail, send the survivor after him.

A party of English officers were lodged in the house of Deacon Elijah Chapman, (now occupied by Daniel Chapman,) and were there while Yorktown was besieged, and a son of Dea. Chapman was a captain of Lafayette's Light Infantry employed in that siege. These officers were always represented by those who remembered them, as making a splendid appearance, and as being very courteous and gentlemanly in their limited intercourse with the inhabitants of the neighborhood.

In concluding the general subject of the revolution, it should be remarked that there were no tories in Tolland. With the exception of two or three odd, crusty, eccentric men, who generally opposed what others approved, and who being in the main respectable persons, whose whimsical opposition was generally amusing, there was entire unanimity in Tolland from the first manifestation of opposition to the tyranny of England until the final establishment of American Independence.

Most of the citizens of Tolland who were conspicuous in the war of the Revolution were the descendants of the first settlers. Among these, the name of CHAPMAN is prominent. They were the descendants of Simon Chapman, who was one of the original proprietors of the town. He lived in Windsor and owned several tracts of land in Tolland, but his son Samuel, (the progenitor of all of the name in the western part of the town,) settled, about the year 1725, on a tract of about forty acres, lying south of a pond called Shenipset pond, deeded to him by John Huntington, of Tolland. To this tract he made great additions from adjacent lands, and his sons still more, until the three brothers, besides out-fields, owned a tract extending two miles or more from south-east to north-west, though of less, but irregular breadth. It was not until about thirty-five years ago that this tract, on which were eight houses, seven of which were of first-class size, and all inhabited by families of the name, began to crumble away and fall into the possession of others. Capt. SAMUEL CHAPMAN, the first settler, (whose decease at Louisburgh has been mentioned,) was grandson of Mr. Edward Chapman, who came from England, settled in Simsbury, and lost his life at the storming of Narraganset Fort in December, 1675. He was the only justice of the peace in Tolland for nine years, and was for eleven years a selectman. Very reliable tradition speaks of him as possessing many estimable qualities, among which was that of being an excellent neighbor. He first lived in a house situated above the entrance of the road that runs south from the fifth district school-house. He then built the house now owned and occupied by Mr. Oliver Eaton, and which, though nearly one hundred and twenty years old, is still in good repair and elegant condition—promising fair to outlive the present century.

Capt. Samuel Chapman had three sons and five daughters, all of whom married and settled in Tolland. The sons became the wealthiest men in the town, and until superannuated, were among the most active, influential, public-spirited citizens.

SAMUEL, eldest son of Capt. Samuel Chapman, was a very eminent citizen, and a very remarkable man. He was a captain in the French war, and colonel of the twenty-second regiment of Connecticut militia during the entire war of the revolution. He was at New York with his regiment in 1776, and when the American forces evacuated that city, his regiment, stationed near Kip's bay, with the brigades of Parsons and Fellows, animated by their colonel, did not participate in the shameful panic of the American troops on that occasion, but made an orderly and honorable retreat. He was also in several other tours of duty; his personal courage and astonishing hardihood were proverbial among his soldiers. His frame and nerves seemed as if made of iron, (for example, he never wore mittens in the coldest weather,) and such was his mental temperament, that disasters which would discourage even superior minds, only aroused his undaunted spirit to more fearless action. Few men could be found so unflinching in moments of danger; and his firmness and energy never faltered under any circumstances. The almost unexampled number of times he was elected a member of the General Assembly, exhibits the regard in which he was held by his townsmen; his was the master spirit that brought the citizens of Tolland into unanimous and energetic action in the revolutionary contest. Col. Chapman was one of the most wealthy men of Tolland, carried on a large business besides farming; would give employment to a poor man who wanted work, regardless of advantage to himself; and even embarrassed his estate by becoming responsible for the debts of the unfortunate.

In person, Col. Chapman was rather under the middle stature, with blue eyes, and his voice was remarkable for its loudness and energy. He was what is called a great reader, was rather taciturn, and of studious habits. He never laughed, and a smile seldom lighted up his austere countenance.

Col. Chapman was born in Windsor, a few years previous to his father's settlement in Tolland; and occupied during his life the house before-mentioned as built by his father. He died March, 1803, aged 83 years, regardless to the last of inclemency of weather or his own personal comfort. He was found dead in his bed. Such was his apparent health and uncomplaining habits, that the disease which occasioned his death, was only a matter of conjecture.

Col. Samuel Chapman married Sarah White, of Bolton, September 20, 1750.

Their children, five in number, were:

Ruth,	born	October 9, 1751.
Sarah,	"	January 15, 1753.
Samuel,	"	April 10, 1755, died July 15, 1756.
Samuel,	"	August 18, 1757, settled in Ellington.

ELIAKIM CHAPMAN, the youngest son of Col. Samuel Chapman, married Roxalana, daughter of Col. Solomon Wills, who died November 24, 1783, after which he married Nancy, the sister of his first wife. He had several children, one of whom, Mrs. Joseph Bishop, is a resident of Tolland. He always resided on his father's farm, was a colonel of militia, representative in the General Assembly, selectman, and a useful citizen.

ELIJAH, second son of Capt. Samuel Chapman, married Sarah Steel, daughter of Rev. Stephen Steel, of Tolland, May 28, 1747. He died —— aged — years. She died ——

Their children, twelve in number, of whom eleven lived to maturity, and most of them to old age, were:

Joanna,	born	May 16, 1748.
Reuben,	"	December 8, 1749.
Sarah,	"	July 23, 1752, died in infancy.
Elijah,	"	July 13, 1753.
Ashbel,	"	June 28, 1755.
Sarah,	"	April 1, 1757.
Ruth,	"	February 20, 1759.
Esther,	"	April 8, 1761.
Roxana,	"	November 14, 1763.
Aaron,	"	September 17, 1765.
Dorcas,	"	September 25, 1767.
Daniel,	"	September 23, 1769.

Of the sons, REUBEN, the oldest, married Mary, daughter of Doct. Samuel Cobb, April 21, 1774, and died October 25, 1776, of consumption, occasioned by hardships suffered while in the revolutionary army, leaving only one child—a son named Solomon, who was born July 3, 1775; whose grandchildren still occupy the lands of their forefathers.

ELIJAH, second son of Dea. Elijah Chapman,—captain in the revolutionary army, sheriff of Tolland county, &c., received an extended notice in the History of Tolland County, published in the Tolland County Record, which it is unnecessary to repeat here. He married Sarah Keeler, of Ridgefield, a lady of unusual worth, and his home and place of his death was in a house (now owned by John Doyle,) which he built on the land of his ancestors. He was the father of Elijah Chapman, first cashier of Tolland County Bank, who united an unusual elegance of manners with an excellent character, and who died at Akron, Ohio, in 1849, aged fifty-nine years.

ASHBEL, third son of Dea. Elijah Chapman, married Miss Lord, of Marlborough, and continued through life on lands received from his father. His sons were: Col. Ashbel Chapman, lately of Tolland, deceased, who always resided on the

THE EARLY HISTORY OF TOLLAND. 65

paternal acres ; Col. Carlos Chapman, now of Windsor Locks; and Col. John B. Chapman, late of Warehouse point, deceased.

AARON, fourth son of Dea. Elijah Chapman, resided during life in the house built by the first Capt. Samuel Chapman, for his son Elijah, father of Aaron, and in which he (Elijah) had resided after marriage, all his life,—the same house being now owned by Daniel, son of Aaron. Dea. Aaron Chapman married a Miss Buel, of Marlborough, and died in December, 1842, aged seventy-seven years, leaving two sons—Novatus and Daniel.

SIMON, youngest son of Capt. Samuel Chapman, married Eunice Preston, April 22, 1762. He died in 1823, aged ninety — years.

Their children were :

Eunice,	born	February 23, 1763.
Simon,	"	June 17, 1764, died December 25, 1767.
Henry,	"	March 31, 1776, died April 11, 1775.
Simon,	"	February 12, 1768.
Nathan,	"	November 5, 1769.
Hannah,	"	August 23, 1773.

Eunice, wife of Simon Chapman, died April 12, 1775. He married for his second wife, Lydia Carlton, of Tolland. Their children were :

Alexander,	born	February 14, 1780.
Jacob,	"	August 29, 1782.
Lydia,	"	July 9, 1784, died July 27, 1784.
Ariel,	"	June 24, 1786.
William,	"	April 19, 1789.
Erastus,	"	April 19, 1792.
Lydia,	"	November 13, 1795.

SARAH, daughter of Capt. Samuel Chapman, married Nathaniel Kingsbury, March 16, 1737, and died July 14, 1794. He died June 23, 1796. Nathaniel Kingsbury was a son of Nathaniel Kingsbury, of Coventry, settled in Tolland about the time of his marriage, on lands granted to him by his father-in-law, and on which his posterity continue to reside. Nathaniel Kingsbury was a deacon of the church in Tolland many years. The children of Nathaniel and Sarah Kingsbury were :

Hannah,	born	January 25, 1738.
Sarah,	"	February 15, 1739.
Three in succession who died in infancy.		
Ruth,	born	October 7, 1750.
Nathaniel,	"	May 5, 1753.
Jabez,	"	March 10, 1756.
Samuel,	"	February 2, 1763.

Jabez, son of Nathaniel and Sarah Kingsbury, married

Anna Hatch, daughter of Joseph Hatch, 2d, August 15, 1776. He died March 25, 1844, aged eighty-eight years. His wife died June 12, 1842, aged eighty-three. Their children were:

Sarah,	born	December 18, 1776.
Mary,	"	January 1, 1778, died February 7, 1778.
John,	"	October 28, 1782.

Jabez Kingsbury was many years deacon of the Congregational church, was a justice of the peace twelve years, was six years a selectman, and was elected to the General Assembly three sessions, discharging his various public and private duties with unusual ability. He was one of the few who can carry on a very extensive farming business with perfect success, and without noise, hurry, or confusion.

Col. John Kingsbury, son of Jabez and Anna, married Sally Dimock, November 1, 1804. She died December 11, 1819, aged 37 years. Second wife, Sally Edgerton, November 1, 1821, who died April 20, 1824. Col. Kingsbury married for his third wife, Mary Brigham of Coventry. Their children are:

John Brigham,	born	October 1, 1826.
George Henry,	"	November 22, 1828.

Col. John Kingsbury died in March, 1861, aged seventy-eight years.

RUTH, daughter of Capt. Samuel Chapman, married Eleazar Steel, as before stated in the notice of the Steel family.

HANNAH, daughter of Capt. Samuel Chapman, married Stephen Steel, Jr., as also previously noticed.

MARGARET, daughter of Capt. Samuel Chapman, married Samuel Ladd, April 28, 1768, and died February 14, 1813. He died May 18, 1814. Their children were:

Ruth,	born	January 18, 1769.
Samuel,	"	May 11, 1770.
Margaret,	"	October 8, 1772.
Mary,	"	November 28, 1775.
Wareham,	"	April 28, 1778.
Jacob,	"	December 14, 1781.

MARY, daughter of Capt. Samuel Chapman, married Solomon Loomis—the date I can not find. She died February 24, 1774, aged forty-two years. Their children were:

Simon,	born	March 7, 1758.
Solomon,	"	September 27, 1760.
Luke,	"	April 11, 1764, died April 27.
Epaphras,	"	September 10, 1768.

The Chapman family has been eminently distinguished in civil as well as military life. Capt. Samuel Chapman, the first settler, was the only justice of the peace in Tolland for nine years, holding the office at the time of his death, and was selectman eleven years.

Col. Samuel Chapman was elected to the General Assembly forty-three times, when the election of members was twice a year, and attended at fifteen special sessions of that body. He was a member of the convention in January, 1788, and voted for the adoption of the present constitution of the United States. He was two years selectman, and twenty-six years, (from 1772 to 1797,) a justice of the peace, when there were but two justices in the town.

Dea. Elijah Chapman, (also captain of militia,) was four times elected to the General Assembly, and eight years selectman.

Gen. Elijah Chapman, (captain in the revolutionary army and major-general of the militia,) was sheriff of Tolland county twenty-three years, and a member of the legislature two sessions. For his biography, see county history.

Capt. Ashbel Chapman was justice of the peace, holding the office at the time of his death, selectman three years, in the Legislature four years, and was a member of the convention in 1818 which formed the present constitution of the state, and voted in the affirmative upon the question of adopting that instrument.

Dea. Aaron Chapman, (of the Baptist church, of which he was the deacon, leader, and principal support for many years previous to his death,) was a selectman three years.

Col. Eliakim Chapman was in the General Assembly one year, and one year a selectman.

Simon Chapman, senior, was selectman two years.

Simon Chapman, Jun., was a captain of militia, a deacon, (which title in those days superseded the other,) and four years a selectman.

Col. Ashbel Chapman, son of Ashbel, was representative one year, and justice of the peace ten years, holding the office at the time of his death.

Col. Carlos Chapman was selectman one year, representative two years, sheriff of Tolland county two years, and four years a justice of the peace.

Novatus Chapman was representative two years, justice of the peace four years, selectman three years, sheriff of Tolland county three years, clerk of the courts one year, and judge of probate for the district of Tolland four years.

For nearly seventy years there has been a family of Chapmans in Tolland, distinct in descent from the foregoing, but descendants from Robert Chapman, one of the earliest and principal settlers of Saybrook. I allude to the late Capt. Ezra Chapman, whose residence was in the village of Sknugamug. He was the son of Ezra Chapman, who was an ensign of Capt. Horton's company of artificers, in Col. Baldwin's regiment in the revolutionary contest, entering the service for the war, August 6, 1777, and continuing therein until his death, September 1, 1778. His only child—Ezra, of Tolland, was born in Hebron, March 26, 1773; was apprenticed to the trade of a blacksmith, (which was that of his father,) and when of age settled in Tolland, where he resided until his death, February 18, 1851, at the age of seventy-eight years. In the apparent enjoyment of his usual health, and while seated at his fireside, he fell into that sleep that knows no waking. Capt. Chapman married Lydia M. Whittlesey, July 6, 1797, by whom he had four children, two of whom still survive, and (with their children and grandchildren,) are citizens of Tolland, viz.: Capt. Sherman Chapman, born January 23, 1803, and Mary, wife of Ansel S. Barber, born March 30, 1805. Mrs. Lydia M. Chapman died December 14, 1806, and Capt. Chapman married for his second wife, Abigail Morgan, May 20, 1809, by whom he had seven children, one of whom, Mrs. Mason Agard, is now a resident of Tolland.

Capt. Ezra Chapman was a man of some prominence. He was quite early made captain of a militia company in Tolland, was a selectman six years, a justice of the peace six years, and a member of the General Assembly two sessions. He was a very industrious man, honest and upright in his dealings, and in every way a worthy citizen. He read more than ordinary men, reflected much, and was very happy in expressing his ideas upon paper. He had a ready pen in drawing the ordinary written agreements used among his neighbors, and excelled in his epistolary efforts—many of his letters bearing marks of thought and scholarship.

WILLS or WILLES. This is one of the names that stand prominent among the early settlers of Tolland. Joshua Wills was an inhabitant of the town of Windsor. His name appears on the petition of the Windsor men for a new township, bearing date May 9, 1713, and presented to the General Assembly at its ensuing session. It also appears as one of the inhabitants of Tolland, on the petition relative to Coventry lands, presented May session, 1718.

The following copy of a petition by Joshua Wills, now among the archives of the state at Hartford, will give some idea of the inhabitants of those times:

"To the Honorable the Governor and Council sitting at Hartford May 25, 1722: The prayer of Joshua Wills of Tolland humbly sheweth: that your poor petitioner, by the holy providence of God, visiting of him with great sickness and of long continuance, is reduced to very hard and low circumstances in the world: my life is still continued to me, through the mercy of God, by my body and my estate brought very low through the force of my disease. I have thought it my duty to repair of the broken state of my health, but have no means that can possibly enable me thereunto. Therefore my humble request is that [you] would give me liberty of a brief to ask charity from christian friends within places and limits as your Honors in your great goodness shall think most suitable: and your petitioner as in duty bound shall pray."

JOSHUA WILLS."

At this time there was a statute prohibiting applications for charitable contributions, without liberty from the governor and council, who were to direct in what towns and societies such briefs should be used. It does not appear what action was had on this petition.

The necessities of the poor and unfortunate were not in those days relieved in this way alone, but they successfully sought relief in other ways. The following extract of a letter from Rev. Stephen Mix, of Wethersfield, to Gov. Talcott, dated May 26, 1726, and the action had thereon, will exhibit the character of the people of that generation in its true light.

"We have," he says, "for a considerable time had many needy persons, (from the eastern towns principally,) coming to us for corn; and they are still daily coming; many that come—perhaps the generality seem to be sober, well disposed persons—showing an honest simplicity and freedom as I imagine from the vices, apt to be found in our more populous and fuller towns :—This evening I hear more of their straits," &c., &c.

This letter occupies a page of foolscap paper, closely written. Gov. Talcott forthwith wrote a message to the Assembly, then in session, on a blank page of this sheet, and forwarded the whole for their consideration. A committee was appointed of members of each house who made a favorable report, and the following resolution was adopted in both houses, to wit:

"May, 1726. This Assembly being informed that there are many persons in the towns of Voluntown, Ashford, Willington, Stafford, Tolland, and Bolton, which by frost in the year past were generally cut short in their crops and thereby are reduced to a suffering, almost a perishing condition :—for the relief of whom this Assembly orders thirty pounds, (one hundred dollars,) money to be drawn out of the public treasury of this colony and to be delivered to Nathaniel Stanley and Ozias Pitkin, who are hereby ordered to send to the several ministers or selectmen of said towns except in Willington; and there to send to John Cady and Thomas Jennings, to inform said committee of such persons as are in a suffering condition; and said committee are hereby ordered to proportion said money to the several towns according to their number and necessities; and said poor persons having a certificate from such ministers, selectmen or others as abovesaid, may repair to such committee who is hereby ordered to deliver unto him or them such support out of the money as they shall see fit."

JOSHUA WILLS was one of the very first persons to whom allotments of land were made in the territory afterwards named Tolland, on the 6th day of February, 1711; and he was one of the original grantees in the deed of the committee who were authorized and empowered to sell the lands in the north part of Tolland. He had a son also named Joshua, who was born before Tolland was settled—the name of Joshua Wills, Jr., appearing on the petition of May 9, 1713.

Joshua Wills, Jr., married Melicent Yeomans, November 9, 1729. She died March 13, 1737. Their children were:

Solomon, born October 14, 1731.
Azariah, " June 27, 1733.
Elizabeth, " May 18, 1735, died July 2, 1736.
Melicent, " March 11, 1737, died March 17, 1737.

Joshua Wills, Jr., married for second wife, Jemima Eaton, August 22, 1739. Their children were:

Elizabeth, born August 14, 1740.
Joshua, " July 15, 1742.
Gideon, " February 1, 1743.
Melicent, " January 12, 1747, died November 19, 1750.

Joshua Wills died August 2, 1767. His widow survived to May 3, 1791. Mr. Wills was a captain of the militia company; a member of the General Assembly thirteen regular and four special sessions; and was selectman thirteen years.

SOLOMON WILLS, son of Joshua and Melicent Wills, married Elizabeth Lathrop, February 24, 1763. She was the daughter of John Lathrop, one of the first settlers in Tolland. Their children were:

Azariah, born May 30, 1772, went to Franklin, N. Y.
Solomon, " January 10, 1775, settled in Pennsylvania.
Wareham, " July 27, 1780. do. do.
Roxalana, " December 3, 1763, first wife of Col. E. Chapman, died November 24, 1780.
Nancy, " September 3, 1765, second wife of Col. E. Chapman.
Elizabeth, " November 30, 1767, married Capt. Ashbel Steel.
Melicent, " September 12, 1769, married Col. Elijah Smith.

Solomon Wills was very early enrolled in the defense of his country. We find his name first as a private soldier in the year 1756, in the French and Indian war. In 1759 he served as a serjeant, in 1758 as an ensign, in 1759 he was a second lieutenant, and in 1762 he was first lieutenant commanding the ill-fated company that went to Cuba, of whom so few returned. In 1775, we find him captain of the volunteer company that performed a tour of duty of eight months, near Boston. The promptness with which this company was formed and made ready for service, speaks well for the character of its commander. The exciting cause of this movement, was the skirmish at Lexington on the 19th of April; and this company of ninety-eight men were at Roxbury, Mass., and mustered into service on the first day of the following May. When we take into consideration the facilities of that day for circulating news or for traveling, this transaction will look the more remarkable. In the campaign of 1776, we find Mr. Wills under the command of Gen. Washington, as a Colonel, in which capacity he served at different periods during the war of the revolution, both in the State and Continental lines. Col. Wills was in civil life also, a very active and useful citizen. He was a selectman of the town three years; a justice of the peace five years; an Associate Judge of Tolland County Court seven years; a member of the General Assembly twenty-three sessions. In 1793 he ceased to act in public life. He died December 10, 1807, aged seventy-six years.

Col. Wills is still represented in Tolland by two ladies, his lineal descendants, viz.: Mrs. Joseph Bishop and Miss Elizabeth S. Kent; they being all the descendants of Joshua Wills, one of the first settlers, now remaining in Tolland.

The name of SAMUEL HUNTINGTON appears on the list of those who died in the service of their country. He was second son of John Huntington, Esq., one of the original grantees of the town of Tolland. John Huntington was from Windsor; was one of the petitioners for the town in May, 1713, though his name does not appear on the subsequent petitions. It is certain that he was of Windsor, January 14, 1719, for on that day he took a deed of John Ellsworth of a tract of land in Tolland containing three hundred acres. He had also a lot of land that was Christopher Huntington's, assigned him November 26, 1719. It is not certain when he moved to Tolland; it is certain, however, he became a resident of this town before April 16, 1723, as there is a record of his marriage on that day as follows: "April 16, 1723. Then was John Huntington of Tolland married to Thankful Warren of Windham." The following is a record of his family:

Thankful,	born	March 16, 1724, died July 14, 1739.
John,	"	February 22, 1725.
Samuel,	"	July 24, 1728.
Andrew,	"	September 17, 1730.
Abigail,	"	October 1, 1732.
Deborah,	"	May 21, 1736.

John Huntington, Esq., died January 26, 1737, aged forty-six years. He was the second justice of the peace ever appointed for the town of Tolland, and he was the only justice from 1733 to his death. He was commissioned as ensign in October, 1723, on the first organization of the militia in Tolland; was one year the town-clerk, and two years selectman—departing this life at almost the commencement of his public usefulness. Tradition assigns his place of residence on the farm now owned and occupied by Dea. Nathan Spalding.

JOHN, the eldest son of John Huntington, Esq., married Mehitabel, daughter of Rev. Stephen Steel, March 23, 1749. The following is their family record:

John,	born	May 14, 1749.
Thankful,	"	July 23, 1750, died October 29, 1750.
Mehitabel,	"	January 24, 1752.
Elisha,	"	December 17, 1754.
William,	"	September 19, 1757.
Hezekiah,	"	December 30, 1759.
Deborah,	"	November 21, 1762.
Samuel,	"	March 23, 1765.
Abigail,	"	March 29, 1767.
Ruth,	"	May 12, 1769.
Thankful.	"	October 3, 1771.
Maria,	"	October 27, 1774, died August 3, 1777.

SAMUEL, second son of John Huntington, Esq., married Jane West, daughter of Deacon Joseph West, December 26, 1751. He was the Ensign in the French war, and died at Lake Onedia, in 1760. His children were:

Thankful,	born	December 24, 1752.
Jane,	"	February 22, 1755.
Diantha,	"	November 4, 1757, died September 20, 1763.
Jerusha,	"	May 1, 1760, died August 5, 1778.

JOHN, son of John and grandson of John Huntington, Esq., married Rebecca Newell, of Ellington, (then East Windsor,) February 20, 1783. Their children were:

John,	born	February 26, 1784, died November 18, 1784.
Mara,	"	February 12, 1786, died May 18, 1787.
John,	"	March 7, 1788.
Frederick Augustus,	"	July 14, 1790.
Ephraim Newell,	"	March 7, 1792, died Febuary 8, 1793.
Rebecca,	"	October 29, 1793.
Mara,	"	June 6, 1795.
Andrew,	"	March 23, 1798.
Robert Goodloe,	"	February 6, 1800.
Almira,	"	February 10, 1802.

ELISHA, son of John and grandson of John Huntington, Esq., married Esther Ladd, June 16, 1785. Their children were:

Andrew,	born	January 25, 1786, died February 8, 1786.
Lucia,	"	May 27, 1787.
Samuel,	"	May 9, 1789.
Ambrose,	"	June 8, 1791.
Esther,	"	September 28, 1793.
Elias,	"	June 6, 1796.
Appollos,	"	November 14, 1798.
Nancy,	"	May 31, 1801.
Laura,	"	May 19, 1804.
Ruth,	"	December 20, 1806.

HEZEKIAH HUNTINGTON, the fourth son of John Huntington and his wife Mehitabel Steel, was in the war of the revolution. At one time he was in an armed ship that made a daring attempt to escape from New London harbor through the British fleet that blockaded the eastern entrance into Long Island sound, but the ship was taken, and the most formidable looking of its men, among them Mr. Huntington, put in irons. He was thus conveyed to New York, and confined in a prison ship, where his sufferings were such as to injure his health during life. He afterwards became an eminent lawyer and politician. For many years he was United States District Attorney for Connecticut, and died in Middletown at an advanced age, leaving children who occupy very prominent places in society, viz.: Samuel H. Huntington, clerk of the court of claims, Washington, D. C., and Hezekiah Huntington, of Hartford.

I am not aware that any of the descendants of John Huntington, Esq., the first settler, are now in Tolland.

Capt. ICHABOD HINCKLEY was the son of Ichabod Hinckley, who came from Barnstable county, Mass., about the year 1732, and settled on the farm now owned by Nathan Pierson. He died May 10, 1768. He was selectman two years. Ichabod Hinckley, Jr., had six children by his first wife, whose name was Mary, viz.: Anna, Bethiah, Temperance, Ichabod, Benjamin, and Daniel. His wife Mary died January 8, 1769. He then married Hannah Kingsbury, daughter of Dea. Nathaniel Kingsbury, for his second wife, December 12, 1769, by whom he had four children, viz.: Mary, Hannah, Sarah, and Deborah. He was a captain in the continental army, and performed several tours of duty, besides being otherwise very active in the revolutionary contest. He was twice a member of the General Assembly, and fourteen years a selectman. People who remembered him used to speak with admiration of his integrity and ability as a selectman, and of the dignity with which he used to preside in town meetings. Capt. Hinckley died February 23, 1807, in his seventy-second year. I do not know that any of his descendants are now in Tolland.

Captain AMOS FELLOWS, of revolutionary memory, was a son of Isaac Fellows, who came from Plainfield, in Windham county, to Tolland about the year 1745. He married Abigail Lathrop, daughter of Ichabod Lathrop, and granddaughter of John Lathrop, who was one of the early settlers in Tolland. The following were his children, viz.:

Ruth,	born	March 27, 1753.
Ichabod,	"	March 7, 1754, died March 18, 1759.
Stephen,	"	April 17, 1755, died June 29, 1759.
Isaac,	"	May 29, 1757.

Abigail, his wife, died June 25, 1773.

Capt Fellows is reported to have been at New York in the twenty-second regiment, in 1776, where he is said to have been taken by the enemy. Certain it is that he was in captivity awhile, and was confined in a prison ship, where his sufferings were the most cruel, and from which he found relief only in the sleep of death. He was said to have been a man of intellect, and of great decision and firmness of character. His death was considered a great loss to the cause, and it was said that had he survived he would have been promoted to a very superior grade. He left only two children, one of whom, Isaac, married and remained in Tolland to the day of his death.

ICHABOD GRIGGS, Jr., was an ensign in the war of the revolution. He was the son of Dea. Ichabod Griggs, who removed from Norwich to Tolland about the year 1744, the year in which his son Ichabod was born. Dea. Ichabod Griggs was representative three sessions, and selectman five years. He died May 9, 1790, aged seventy-two years. His children were as follows:

Joshua,	born	January 8, 1743, at Norwich.
Ichabod,	"	June 7, 1744.
Sarah,	"	June 6, 1749.

JOSHUA, eldest son of Dea. Ichabod Griggs, was, like his father, a deacon in the church and a very respectable man. He was an adjutant in the revolutionary service, and was a selectman five years. He married Joanna, daughter of Dea. Elijah Chapman, December 11, 1766. Their children were:

Roswell,	born	September 23, 1767.
Joshua,	"	June 17, 1769.
Susannah,	"	January 30, 1771.
Daniel,	"	April 15, 1773.
Charles,	"	August 15, 1775.
Sarah,	"	September 23, 1777.
Elijah,	"	September 5, 1780.
Joanna,	"	September 5, 1783.

Dea. Joshua Griggs died June 9, 1813, aged seventy years.

Roswell, eldest son of Dea. Joshua Griggs, married Sarah Dunham, of Mansfield, October 27, 1791. The following are their children, to wit:

Mary,	born	May 15, 1792.
Sally,	"	March 5, 1794.
Minerva,	"	August 6, 1796, married Doct. O. K. Isham, November 12, 1822.
Charles,	"	April 14, 1799.
Eunice Hovey,	"	August 27, 1801.
Elijah Chapman,	"	September 5, 1803, died January 23, 1806.
Roswell Leonard,	"	March 11, 1806, died April 6, 1815.
Seth Dunham,	"	May 1, 1809
Parmela Porter,	"	August 13, 1812, died February 3, 1813.
Julia,	"	March 17, 1814.
Normand Brigham,	"	June 18, 1816.

Joshua, son of Dea. Joshua Griggs, was a physician, and for a short time practiced in Tolland, but removed to the west.

Daniel, son of Dea. Joshua Griggs, married Nancy Pinney, of Ellington, January 19, 1806. The following are their children, viz.:

Joshua,	born	October 11, 1806.
Eliza,	"	February 19, 1808.
Lucius,	"	January 9, 1810.
Harriet,	"	November 28, 1811, died March 1, 1815.
Daniel,	"	March 2, 1814.
Harriet,	"	May 27, 1816.
Lemuel P.,	"	May 19, 1818.
Henry O.,	"	March 30, 1821.
Charles G.,	"	November 25, 1823.
James Randolph,	"	May 7, 1827.

Ensign Ichabod Griggs, son of Dea. Ichabod Griggs, married Mary Hatch, daughter of Joseph Hatch, the second, December 19, 1765. He died at New Rochelle, N. Y., September 30, 1776, aged thirty-two years. His children were:

Joseph,	born	January 30, 1767.
Samuel,	"	May 10, 1768.
Stephen,	"	October 3, 1769.
Anna,	"	September 14, 1773, died April 23, 1787.
Matta,	"	February 12, 1777.

Samuel Griggs, son of Ichabod and Mercy Griggs, married Mary Hinckley, daughter of Capt. Ichabod Hinckley, all of Tolland, February 16, 1792. His children were:

Anna,	born	October 6, 1792.
Ichabod,	"	February 28
Chester,	"	April 6.

Stephen Griggs, son of Ichabod and Mercy Griggs, married Betsey Lathrop, daughter of Solomon Lathrop, and a niece of Hope Lathrop, March 8, 1792. His children were:

Harriet,	born	December 27, 1792.
Chauncey,	"	April 10, 1796.
Ralph,	"	January 31, 1798.
Solomon Lathrop,	"	April 7, 1800.
Austin,	"	July 26, 1805.
Leverett,	"	November 6, 1808.

The descendants of Dea. Joshua Griggs, now residents in Tolland, are Mrs. Mary Cowen, Mrs. Oliver K. Isham, and Mr. Joshua Griggs. They are also descendants of Deacon Elijah Chapman, through Joanna, wife of Dea. Joshua Griggs.

The descendants of Ichabod Griggs, 2d, are descendants of Joseph Hatch, one of the first settlers in Tolland, through Mercy, wife of said Ichabod.

The descendants of Stephen Griggs are descendants also of Hope Lathrop, one of the first settlers in Tolland, through Betsey, wife of said Stephen Griggs.

Ichabod Griggs, 1st, was representative in the General Assembly three sessions, and selectman five years.

Stephen Griggs was selectman one year, and captain of a militia company.

Chauncey Griggs was representative in the General Assembly two sesssions, judge of the Probate Court for the district of Tolland two years, and a justice of the peace fourteen years.

Ralph R. Griggs was a justice of the peace five years.

Solomon Lathrop Griggs, was sheriff of Tolland county six years, and selectman four years.

Seth D. Griggs and Joshua Griggs, were each representatives in the General Assembly one session.

JAMES CHAMBERLIN commanded a company of cavalry one or two tours of duty during the war of the revolution. He came to Tolland from Coventry about the year 1772, and removed to East Windsor before the year 1782. While in this town he lived at the extreme south-east part of it, on a farm lying east of the one lately owned by Jesse West. He was one of the representatives from Tolland in the General Assembly, October session, 1775 ; otherwise I can learn nothing more of him than that he was a revolutionary officer.

The name of JOSEPH BAKER frequently occurs as one who actively participated in the early settlement of Tolland. He was one of the petitioners in 1713, for a charter of the new town, and his name is on various other petitions relative to its settlement ; he also received an early allotment of land. He was one of the fifty-one grantees of the township in 1719. He was of Windsor and was the grandson of Jeffrey Baker, from England, one of the early settlers of that town. Joseph Baker finally removed his entire family, (all of whom were born in Windsor,) to Tolland, in the year 1724. He settled on a tract of several hundred acres lying south of Shenipset pond,—he was a large landholder, owning besides other tracts, one in the south-west district, where he settled two or three of his sons, and where their descendants have resided until this day. One of his sons, Jacob, was educated for the ministry and graduated at Yale College in 1731, being the earliest graduate belonging to Tolland ; but he was consumptive—never preached except where there was a temporary vacancy, and died early in life. Joseph Baker was two years a selectman, and died in 1784, aged seventy-five years. His son, John, married Sarah, daughter of Dea. Isaac Davis, of Windsor; settled on his share of the original tract, near Shenipset pond, and died in 1802, at the age of ninety-five years. Jerusha, his only child who lived to maturity, married Samuel Stanley;—their oldest son, John Stanley, born in 1752, married Abigail Gibbs, of East Windsor, in 1771 ;—their oldest son, Roswell Stanley, born in 1772, died in 1850, aged seventy-eight years, on the land of his ancestors ;—the farm being now occupied by Col. Sanford Stanley, and was formerly the residence of Sidney Stanley, Esq., now of Hartford, who during his employment at the office of Secretary of State, furnished me with copies of documents in the public archives, relative to the history of this town. And I take pleasure in publicly acknowledging my obligations to Mr. Stanley for many of the interesting facts and incidents used in this history, and would recommend those who may desire further information upon this subject, to avail themselves of his extensive research and fund of facts relative to the early settlers of Tolland.

JOSEPH BAKER, Jr., married Margaret Gibbs, of East Windsor, January, 21, 1731. Their children were:

Seth,	born	July 2, 1733.
Titus,	"	June 18, 1736.
Joseph,	"	November 18, 1738.
Ebenezer,	"	February 8, 1740.
Mary,	"	August 5, 1745.
Daniel,	"	January 6, 1747, died June 3, 1752.
Ruth,	"	December 25, 1749.

THE EARLY HISTORY OF TOLLAND.   79

JOSEPH BAKER, son of Joseph Baker, Jr., married Lois Carpenter, March 25, 1762. He was the father of Alvin Baker and Eli Baker, who lived and died in the south-west part of Tolland. Eli Baker was three years a selectman and four years a member of the General Assembly.

Heman, son of Joseph Baker, senior, settled on his father's homestead, married Lois Gilbert, of Hebron, and died in 1805, aged eighty-six years. The children of Heman and Lois Gilbert were:

Heman,	born	October 11, 1748.
Ann,	"	April 24, 1750.
Deborah,	"	January 12, 1752.
John,	"	January 26, 1754.
Oliver,	"	October 5, 1755.
Abigail,	"	November 5, 1757.
Lois,	"	November 14, 1760.
Delight,	"	December 21, 1762.
Lydia,	"	February 4, 1765.

HEMAN BAKER, Jr., was a sergeant in Capt. Solomon Wills' company of volunteers at Roxbury, in 1775. The next year he was taken prisoner, together with his brother-in-law, Joel Smith, near New York, and after being kept in the usual severe confinement, they were exchanged or released, and having been unnecessarily and maliciously exposed to the small pox, they were permitted to return to their homes. On their way they became ill, and were unable to proceed farther than East Hartford, where it was discovered that they both had the small pox in the most malignant form, and where they both died. Heman Baker, Jr., died January 21, 1777. He was a single man. Joel Smith left a widow and two small children. Their grave-stones yet remain where they were buried,—not in the public burying ground, but in a field near the house in which they died. No one of their friends in Tolland could be present during their sickness or burial.

Oliver Baker became a physician and settled in New Hampshire.

NOTE.—This family should not be confounded with that of a Mr. Heman Baker, who moved into Tolland from Massachusetts, and some of whose descendants for a generation or two, continued in the eastern section of the town.

JOHN BAKER, son of Heman Baker, Sen., married Elizabeth Dimick, July 22, 1779. Their family record is as follows:

Celinde,	born	April 22, 1780, married Hon. E. Stearns, November 4, 1800.
Nancy,	"	May 5, 1782.
Almira,	"	April 16, 1784.
Amelia,	"	June 10, 1786.
Seymour,	"	June 25, 1788.
Lydia,	"	October 25, 1790.
Chauncey,	"	September 18, 1794.
Florilla,	"	October 17, 1797.

John Baker married for his second wife, Alice Jewett, December 25, 1806. They had one child, Juliana, born September 10, 1809.

The name "Joseph Baker," which was the name of the first Baker who settled in Tolland, has been continued in a direct line for more than two hundred years, and is now borne by a young man who is the seventh in unbroken succession.

Two persons by the name of BENTON died in the service of their country in the French and revolutionary wars, viz.: WILLIAM BENTON, who died at Oswego in August, 1760; and AZARIAH BENTON, who died in captivity in a prison ship in Long Island sound, December 29, 1776. They were lineal descendants of Samuel Benton, Sen., who was formerly of Hartford, in this state.

Samuel Benton, Sen., was one of the grantees in the deed of the committee to the first proprietors of Tolland. There were in that deed four grantees by the name of Benton, viz.: Samuel Benton, Sen., Samuel Benton, Jr., Joseph Benton, Sen., and Joseph Benton, Jr. The name of Daniel Benton appears first as one of the twenty-five petitioners respecting the Coventry lands in May, 1718. On the 20th day of February, 1719, Samuel Benton, describing himself of Hartford, gave a deed of land situated in Tolland, to Daniel Benton, also of Hartford, which deed is expressed to be "in consideration of love and good will I have and do have unto my loving son Daniel Benton," &c., &c. The land is described as containing forty acres; be the same more or less, &c., &c. On the 23d day of May, 1719, he had a lot of land surveyed to him, north-westerly from Skungamug pond. On the 20th day of June, 1719, he had another tract set to him which had a highway across it, leading from the highway that run west from James Stimson's. This tract was doubtless on both sides of the highway that runs from the south burying ground southwestward to the saw mill. July 25, 1721, he had other lots

THE EARLY HISTORY OF TOLLAND. 81

surveyed to him—one of which was estimated at seventy acres, and one twenty-seven acres.

Daniel Benton married Mary Skinner, January 3, 1722. They had three sons, viz. :

Daniel,	born	January 6, 1723.
William,	"	November 12, 1725.
Elijah,	"	June 30, 1728.

WILLIAM BENTON'S name is upon the roll of Capt. Samuel Stoughton, in the year 1757, at the time the French took fort William Henry; also upon the roll of Capt. Samuel Chapman, in the year 1758. He married Sarah Burroughs, December 14, 1750, by whom he had one son, John, born March 2, 1754. They had three daughters, whose names were Sarah, Ruth, and Abigail. William Benton died at Oswego in the month of August, 1760, aged thirty-four years.

DANIEL, son of Daniel and Mary Benton, married Mary Wheeler, November 3, 1747. They had seven sons, as follows:

Elisha,	born	August 9, 1747, died January 21, 1777.
Daniel,	"	April 29, 1748.
Azariah,	"	March 29, 1752, died in a prison ship, 1776.
Jacob,	"	April 22, 1754.
William,	"	April 13, 1760.
Nathan,	"	May 3, 1764.
Silas,	"	June 6, 1766.

DANIEL, son of Daniel Benton and Mary Wheeler, his wife, married Betty Richards, of Somers, February 18, 1779. Their children were:

Elisha,	born	March 20, 1780.
Betty,	"	March 20, 1782.
Eunice,	"	July 23, 1784.
Agnes,	"	February 12, 1787, died August 19, 1791.
Phebe,	"	August 12, 1791.

EUNICE married Bliss Chapin, of Somers, and occupied the family homestead where their son, Theodore Chapin, now resides.

JACOB BENTON, the son of Daniel Benton and Mary Wheeler, his wife, married Sarah Weston, of Willington, March 14, 1782. They had two children, Anna, born February 1, 1783, and William, born August 29, 1785. Mrs. Benton died September 23, 1787. He married for his second wife, Sarah, daughter of Jonathan Ladd, Jr., of Tolland, January 1, 1789. Their children were:

Azariah,	born	June 8, 1790.
Ruth,	"	December 8, 1791.
Daniel,	"	May 3, 1794.
Susalla,	"	February 19, 1796.
Chester,	"	February 5, 1798.
Jacob,	"	June 1, 1802.

Jacob Benton was a revolutionary soldier. At the age of only seventeen he was a dragoon in the army that captured Burgoyne, and saw the forces of that officer march off as prisoners. He died in 1843, at the age of eighty-three.

AZARIAH, eldest son of Jacob and Sarah Benton, and now deceased, was a deacon of the Congregational church, and the father of Rev. William A. Benton, missionary to Syria; also of Azariah L. Benton, a resident of Tolland.

DANIEL, son of Jacob Benton, and his children, are also residents of this town.

Samuel Benton, Jr., was one of the grantees in the first deed of Tolland, and probably was the son or grandson of Samuel Benton, Sen., first above-mentioned. He married Jane Bradley, December 22, 1743. Their children were:

Elihu,	born	December 26, 1744.
Jonathan,	"	September 9, 1746.
Ozias,	"	February 25, 1748.
Samuel,	"	May 9, 1757.
Zadoc,	"	March 7, 1761.
Jacob,	"	September 30, 1768.
Thankful,	"	April —, 1751, burned to death in a house destroyed by fire, Nov., 1751.
Thankful,	"	August 22, 1752.
Dorothy,	"	February 23, 1755.
Sarah,	"	December 21, 1764.

Ozias, son of Samuel and Jane Benton, married Sarah Day, of East Windsor, (now Ellington,) November 19, 1772. Their children were:

Solomon,	born	May 1, 1775.
Adonijah,	"	May 25, 1777.
Ozias,	"	January 1, 1781.
Ira,	"	September 16, 1783.
Alvin,	"	May 21, 1786.
Alfred,	"	January 6, 1789.
Benjamin D.,	"	June 14, 1791.
Levi,	"	February 6, 1794.

In the year 1816, a disease, called by physicians "congestive pneumonia," made its appearance in Tolland, and in six weeks time occasioned the death of sixteen persons, all of them adults. Only one man recovered who was taken with it. In the family of Ozias Benton the deaths were as follows:

Ozias, senior,	died	March 21, 1816.
Benjamin D., son of Ozias,	"	" 21, "
Sarah, wife of Ozias, senior,	"	" 24, "
Adonijah, son of Ozias,	"	" 24, "
Ozias, Jr., son of Ozias,	"	" 26, "

ADONIJAH, son of Ozias and Jane Benton, married Anna Post, of Tolland, November 23, 1803. Their children were:

Erastus,	born	January 17, 1805.
Austin,	"	November 14, 1806.

THE EARLY HISTORY OF TOLLAND.   83

Benjamin D.,   born   February 22, 1809.
George B.,   "   May 23, 1811.
Juliana,   "   October 17, 1813.

Benjamin D. Benton is a resident of Tolland.

ALVIN BENTON, son of Ozias and Jane, married Ruth, daughter of S. R. Kingsbury, and great granddaughter of Rev. Stephen Steel, March 24, 1812.

TIMOTHY BENTON was undoubtedly a relative of the families already described, but the precise relationship I am unable to determine. The first Timothy Benton found upon our records, married Abigail Scott, of Tolland, June 29, 1738. Their children were:

Abigail,   born   November 1, 1740.
Eleanor,   "   August 12, 1742.
Mehitabel,   "   April 21, 1745.
Elizabeth,   "   February 21, 1747.
Prudence,   "   March 12, 1749.
Huldah,   "   July 15, 1751.
Jerusha,   "   March 22, 1753.
Timothy,   "   August 2, 1755.

TIMOTHY, son of Timothy and Abigail Benton, was in the revolutionary service; and afterwards on the establishment of an artillery company in Tolland, at the first choice of officers, was elected its captain. He possessed an unusually excellent common school education, and was a popular school-master. Capt. Benton resided in the large house near the north-west burying ground, now owned by the heirs of Milton Webster, where he died April 18, 1816, of the "congestive pneumonia," above-mentioned. He married Sarah, daughter of Joseph West, of Tolland, November 9, 1780. Their son, Timothy, lately deceased, was born March 3, 1786;—his first wife was Minerva Webster, of Tolland. The sons of Timothy and Minerva Benton were: Milton W. (lately deceased,) born December 16, 1812; Charles West, born July 7, 1814.

JOSEPH BENTON, one of the grantees in the first deed, was the first town-clerk of Tolland, and held the office three years, or from 1717 to 1720; but he was a poor penman as his records will show. He was a selectman two years, and was otherwise entrusted with public affairs. I can not find any record of his family, nor do I know whether he had one. He was one of the first deacons of the church in Tolland, and in the final settlement of the line between Coventry and Tolland, was located in the former town.

WILLIAM EATON was one of the victims of the campaign of 1762. He was the grandson of William Eaton, one of the first settlers in Tolland. William Eaton the first, was from the town of Windsor. He was one of the petitioners of May, 1718, respecting Coventry lands; he had lands surveyed to him on the 18th day of May, and 29th of December, 1719, and 28th November, 1720. All these lands were in the south part of the town, and bounded on Skungamug river. He was born December 15, 1665, and married Mary Burnet, January 11, 1693. The following is the record of this family:

Daniel,	born	December 7, 1693, died July 20, 1716.
Mary,	"	March 23, 1695.
Ebenezer,	"	November 29, 1697, died June 17, 1716.
William,	"	July —, 1700, one Monday in pease time.
Samuel,	"	September 11, 1705.
Bethiah,	"	November 3, 1708.

The first William Eaton was the first selectman ever chosen in Tolland. He was elected in the year 1717, and re-elected the two succeeding years.

William, son of William and Mary Eaton, married a woman whose Christian name was Rachel. Their children were:

Ebenezer,	born	January 6, 1727, died August 1, 1728.
Juda,	"	March 10, 1728-9.
Rachel,	"	November 15, 1730.
William,	"	October 17, 1732, died at Havana.
Jemima,	"	January 26, 1735.
Peter,	"	August 19, 1737, died November 25, 1752.

WILLIAM, son of William and Rachel Eaton, married Lydia Cook, November 13, 1754. Their family record is as follows:

Ann,	born	November 17, 1755.
Solomon,	"	December 24, 1757.
William,	"	June 24, 1759, died October 12, 1760.
Epaphras,	"	August 8, 1761.

This William Eaton was one of the men who went in the expedition to the Island of Cuba in 1762. He was taken with the fever that proved fatal to so many of the troops about the time the army was to leave the island. Mr. Eaton was taken to the beach preparatory to embarking, and was left by his attendants who returned to bring some things he needed, but when they came back they found he had expired. They had no time to spare and buried him in the sand where he died.

SOLOMON EATON, son of William and Lydia Eaton, married Elizabeth Delano, daughter of Sylvanus Delano, and granddaughter of Jonathan Delano, who will receive further notice under the title of "Town Clerks." They were married June 23, 1777. The following is their family record:

Jasper,	born	January 26, 1781.
Zerad,	"	November 30, 1783.
Luther,	"	November 24, 1785.
Ralph,	"	January 23, 1788.
Clarissa,	"	December 2, 1789.
Sally,	"	December 21, 1791.
Almandor,	"	January 15, 1794.
Anna,	"	July 3, 1796, married David Johnson, December 18, 1716.

Solomon Eaton was one of the revolutionary veterans of Tolland. He served during nearly the entire war, and was in many engagements. It is to be regretted that the full service of any of those men can not now be ascertained. At Monmouth, Mr. Eaton was slightly wounded, and in that battle he killed a British grenadier in fair single-handed conflict during a charge with bayonets,—a necessity on which, in a conversation with a friend of the writer in his broken old age, his mind seemed to dwell with sadness. Mr. Eaton was in Lafayette's light infantry;—in September, 1824, when that distinguished individual had just commenced his celebrated tour through this country, Mr. Eaton had the satisfaction of an interview with his former commander. It was at the brick tavern in the east part of Vernon. The friend before referred to witnessed their parting. As they shook hands, Mr. Eaton said : "I wish you a pleasant journey." "God bless you," replied the General. Mr. Eaton was esteemed as the best soldier of the veteran company in which he served his longest term, and enjoyed through life a higher soldierly renown than any other of the rank and file furnished by Tolland. His patriotic feelings during life were very exalted. He worshiped his country and its emblems. One of his descendants, Horatio D. Eaton, of Hartford, is now an officer of the Connecticut volunteers.

Solomon Eaton died in September, 1843, at the age of eighty-five years, being the last survivor but one of the revolutionary soldiers in Tolland.

The descendants of William Eaton, who died at Havana, remaining in this town, are those of his son Solomon, viz.: Luther Eaton, Esq., and family, Mrs. Anna Johnson, widow of David Johnson, and family, Mrs. A. M. Hawkins and her children, and Oliver, son of Ralph Eaton, now residing on the original Chapman homestead. Several of the descendants of Solomon Eaton reside in Hartford.

Other persons of the name of Eaton were among the first settlers of Tolland; one of whom, Thomas Eaton, came from Woodstock and settled here in the year 1721. He had two twin sons born on the first day of March, 1739, whom he named Moses and Aaron. Moses died in 1739, and there is no record of the family after that date. Thomas Eaton's wife's name was Elizabeth Parker. They were married December 7, 1721. Their son Aaron was twenty-three years old at the time of the Cuba expedition, and as one Aaron Eaton of Lieut. Wills' company died in that expedition, I think the conclusion reasonable that he was the son of Thomas Eaton of Tolland.

Samuel, the son of William and Mary Eaton, married a wife whose name was Jemima—the surname not given. Their children were:

Jemima,	born	May 8, 1732.
Bethiah,	"	January 14, 1733.
Samuel,	"	September 15, 1734.
Aaron,	"	March 8, 1737.

Samuel Eaton, Sen., died in 1737. His son, Aaron, might have been the one in the Cuba expedition, but being a relative of the William Eaton who was in that expedition, and as there is no family tradition that William had any relative in the same service, I have supposed the other Aaron Eaton was the one who went to Cuba.

CONSTANT CRANDAL was another of the victims of the Cuba expedition. He came to Tolland probably after the year 1750. There is no record of him or his family other than that he had a son born July 25, 1757, and that he died at Havana, August 27, 1762. Giles Crandal came into town about the same time. He had a son, Samuel, who married Bethiah Eaton, August 12, 1749. Probably she was the daughter of Samuel and Jemima Eaton. They had thirteen children, among whom was one named Samuel, who was born April 13, 1774, who married Roxana Rawdon, November 23, 1792, and they were the parents of the late Jarvis Crandal, who died June 28, 1854, and who is long to be remembered as one of the sweet singers in Israel; also of Amos Crandal now of this town. These Crandal families are of course the descendants of William Eaton, the first settler of that name in Tolland.

NOAH STIMPSON or Stimson was another of the young men of Tolland who died on the Island of Cuba. He was the grandson of Doct. James Stimson, who was the first physician located in Tolland. James Stimson, before 1716, resided in Lynn, Essex county, Massachusetts. He married Hannah Stearns, a sister of Shubael Stearns and John Stearns, two of the first settlers in Tolland, at Lynn, March 21, 1710. He must have removed to Tolland before March 22, 1716, for his daughter Hannah is recorded as born in Tolland on that day. He was one of the twenty-five inhabitants of Tolland who signed the petition of May, 1718, to the General Assembly, respecting the Coventry lands. He had allotments of land made to him on the 21st of June, 1720, and received a deed of land from Samuel Benton, Jr., dated December 4, 1721. The residence of Doct. Stimpson was near the spot now occupied by Mr. George Morgan. He died March 10, 1758—one hundred and three years ago; therefore I can obtain no information relative to his repute in his profession; only the records abundantly show that he was in the medical practice.

JAMES STIMSON's eldest son, Ichabod, was born in Lynn, Mass., January 22, 1713, and married Margaret Pack, daughter of Joseph Pack, another of the first settlers of the town, February 28, 1740. Their first son, Stephen, was born November 5, 1740; married Keziah, daughter of John Paulk, November 26, 1767. Their first daughter, Jane, was born March 27, 1772. She married Joshua Luce of Tolland, and they were the parents of Leverett Luce, lately of this town, and owner of what was called Luce's mills.

The following is the record of Doct. James Stimson's family:

Ichabod,	born	January 22, 1713.
Eneas,	"	May 25, 1714.
Hannah,	"	March 22, 1716.
James,	"	September 20, 1719.
Naomi,	"	November 8, 1722.
Thomas,	"	July 26, 1725.

The children of Ichabod and Margaret Stimson were:

Stephen,	born	November 5, 1740.
Noah,	"	October 14, 1742, died at Havana.
Sarah,	"	October 5, 1744.
Joseph,	"	January 12, 1746.
Ruth,	"	May 1, 1749.
Joel,	"	July 31, 1751
Margaret,	"	November 25, 1753.
Lois,	"	January 22, 1756.
Alice,	"	February 12, 1758.
Gideon,	"	September 13, 1761.
Eneas,	"	February 17, 1765.

THOMAS, the youngest son of Doct. James Stimson, married Hannah Flint, February 11, 1747. Their children were as follows:

Aaron,	born	November 28, 1749.
John,	"	September 1, 1751.
Hannah,	"	May 17, 1754.
Simon,	"	December 2, 1756.
Abel,	"	March 20, 1762.
David,	"	April 14, 1764.
Miriam,	"	October 25, 1766.
Ruth,	"	September 3, 1769.
Joshua,	"	May 14, 1772.

Thomas Stimson died January 24, 1796, aged seventy-one.

JOSHUA, youngest child of Thomas Stimson, was the father of Mrs. Sarah Northrop, at present a resident of Tolland, and a descendant of two of the first settlers, to wit: Doct. James Stimson and Joseph Pack.

Among the names of those who went from Tolland to Cuba in 1762, is that of JOHN BARNARD, who never returned. He was the son of Doct. Thomas Barnard, the second physician that ever located in this town. Doct. Barnard was from Hadley, Mass., and took a deed from James Lassell, dated April 12, 1734, describing a tract of land lying on both sides of the Skungamug river, a little south of Cook's bridge. This was doubtless the farm now owned and occupied by Doct. Jeduthan C. Eaton, which farm it is known he occupied for some time. Probably Dr. Barnard came to Tolland at about the date of Lassell's deed. He had four sons whose names were, Moses, born Feb. 16, 1729; John, born Aug. 6, 1731; Samuel, born May 13, 1737; and Aaron, born Sept. 30, 1746. He died in 1780, aged seventy-three years. Some of the aged people, with whom I formerly had conversation respecting the early history of the town, recollected Dr. Barnard as a very respectable gentleman, and a good doctor. He did not, however, make any very prominent mark, nor do the records show that he was actively engaged in any public business. Moses, his eldest son, married Ann Loomis, daughter of Solomon

Loomis, May 22, 1750. The following is the record of this family.

Francis,	born	August 31, 1750, died February 10, 1774
Esther,	"	November 20, 1752, died December 12, 1773.
Jonathan,	"	February 27, 1755.
Ann,	"	August 23, 1757, died February 21, 1774.
Moses,	"	January 28, 1760.
William,	"	September 22, 1764.
John,	"	June 26, 1766, died January 26, 1774.
Reuben,	"	October 24, 1768.
Abby,	"	February 20, 1771.
Solomon,	"	November 30, 1772, died February 10, 1773.

Ann, the wife of Thomas Barnard, died Jan. 12, 1774.

It will be seen that there were five deaths in this family between Dec. 12, 1773 and Feb. 25, 1774, a period of only seventy-one days—a mother and four children. Moses Barnard, the father, died at New Rochelle, N. Y., in the service of his country, Oct. 15, 1776, aged forty-six years.

I have no knowledge that any of the descendants of Doct. Barnard are now in Tolland; but as two of their number, while belonging in town, lost their lives in the service of their country, the family ought ever to have a place in the town's history.

The Hatch family also lost a member in the expedition to Cuba. Judah Hatch, of Tolland, died at Havana in 1762. He was the son of Ichabod Hatch, who came from Falmouth, Barnstable Co., Mass., in the year 1726, and whose wife's name was Abigail Works. Their children were:

Zerviah,	born	October 5, 1715.
Joseph,	"	August 18, 1718.
Judah,	"	November 11, 1720.
Justus,	"	October 20, 1722.
Abigail,	"	March 27, 1725.
Daniel,	"	September 24, 1726.
Ruth,	"	August 15, 1729.
Ichabod,	"	October 28, 1732.

The name of Hatch is associated intimately with the settlement of the town. Joseph Hatch was one of the grantees in the first deed from the Windsor committee, and is one of the petitioners respecting the Coventry lands in 1718. He probably lived in Windsor before 1713, but there is reason to believe he removed to Tolland in that year, and was one of the first two, if not the very first, permanent settler in the town of Tolland. A record of his family was made May 26, 1722, in Tolland, commencing in these words:

"Joseph Hatch, a record of his children's births and deaths

in Tolland, in the county of Hartford, in the colony of Connecticut, in New England.

Amy Hatch, daughter of Joseph Hatch, was born October 10, 1713.
Joseph Hatch, the son of Joseph Hatch, was born on September 12, 1715."

Tradition says that this was the first male child born in Tolland.

Mercy,	born	August 23, 1717.
Jonathan,	"	September 29, 1718.

Children of Joseph Hatch and Rebecca, his second wife.

Lemuel,	born	February 29, 1735.
Rebecca,	"	June 8, 1737, died September 14, 1739.
Ebenezer,	"	April 21, 1740.
Timothy,	"	August 14, 1741.

This Joseph Hatch was two years a selectman, and was the first tavern-keeper in Tolland, being chosen a tavern-keeper at a town meeting Jan. 6th, 1718. He was the first military officer in Tolland, having been commissioned a lieutenant in Oct., 1722, and captain in May, 1725. He was the owner of the land in the south part of Tolland, now in the ownership of Frank Hatch, his great grandson; which has always been in the possession of the family since the first settlement of the town, a period of one hundred and forty-eight years.

Joseph, son of the above Joseph Hatch, married Mary Clark, of Lebanon, March 10, 1741. He died February 23, 1773, aged fifty-eight years. His children were:

Mary,	born	January 15, 1742.
Jonathan,	"	September 24, 1743.
Mercy,	"	February 28, 1746.
William,	"	December 28, 1747, died March 26, 1777, at Natham, New Jersey.
Joseph,	"	April 13, 1750.
Abithea,	"	May 12, 1753.
Bethiah,	"	January 13, 1755.
Dan,	"	December 29, 1757.
Anna,	"	September 18, 1759.
Timothy,	"	February 1, 1761.
Isaac and Rebecca,	"	May 24, 1763.

Joseph Hatch, 3d, son of Joseph 2d, married Sarah Parks, Sept. 18, 1772.

Joseph, their son, was born		January 9, 1773.
Betsey,	"	August 27, 1774.
Anna,	"	September 24, 1776.
Sally,	"	October 24, 1778.
William,	"	December 31, 1780, died July 2, 1709.
Ephraim,	"	March 21, 1783.
Ruth,	"	July 20, 1785.
Dana,	"	January 3, 1788, died March 16, 1792.
Frank,	"	April 28, 1790.
Dana,	"	February 19, 1795.

Abner Hatch was a resident of Tolland before 1747, and on Nov. 5, of that year, married Abigail Loomis, daughter of

Solomon Loomis, one of the early settlers of the town. Their children were:

Jerusha,	born	May 22, 1748.
Abigail,	"	February 4, 1750.
Abner,	"	January 31, 1753.
Eleazar,	"	August 29, 1755, died June 12, 1763.
Hannah,	"	February 12, 1758.
Edy,	"	September 20, 1760.
Esther,	"	February 10, 1763.
Eleazar,	"	September 17, 1769.
Sarah,	"	February 3, 1768.

The children of Edy, son of Abner Hatch were:

Experience,	born	September 14, 1722.
Abner,	"	November 22, 1726.
Hannah,	"	January 15, 1729.
Sarah,	"	April 10, 1734.
David,	"	February 8, 1736.
Lucy,	"	August 4, 1740.

Eleazar Hatch married Thankful, daughter of Joseph Lathrop, December 31, 1767. Their children were:

Semantha,	born	November 22, 1768.
Morana,	"	June 1, 1770.
Zadoc,	"	January 6, 1772.
Nathaniel,	"	January 19, 1774, died August 6, 1803.
Prudence,	"	June 8, 1776.
Grace,	"	April 3, 1778, died October 22, 1800.
Jeduthan,	"	December 20, 1780.
Lectana,	"	April 15, 1785.

Mrs. Thankful Hatch, wife of Eleazar, died March 17, 1803.

Zadoc, son of Eleazar and Thankful Hatch, married Caroline Holbrook, June 13, 1793. The following is a record of their family:

Gustin,	born	November 3, 1794, died September 28, 1796.
Nersa,	"	January 21, 1796, died September 3, 1798.
Marvin,	"	November 13, 1797, died February 15, 1813.
Grace,	"	October 18, 1800.
Lectana,	"	September 13, 1802.
Caroline,	"	October 11, 1804.
Mary Hyde,	"	May 20, 1806, died February 22, 1808.
Lovisa,	"	September 14, 1807.
Eleazar Lathrop,	"	November 18, 1809.

Jonathan, son of the second Joseph Hatch, married Bathsheba, daughter of Dea. Joseph West, December 5, 1765. Their children were:

Bathsheba,	born	June 15, 1768.
Mary,	"	May 5, 1770.
Clarissa,	"	October 27, 1772.
Jonathan,	"	August 24, 1774.

Mrs. Bathsheba Hatch died September 1, 1774, and Jonathan Hatch married for his second wife, Mary, daughter of Daniel Benton, Jr., April 28, 1777. Their children were:

Jerusha,	born	June 6, 1778.
Rosamond,	"	May 11, 1780.
Asenath,	"	May 6, 1782.
Mary,	"	April 19, 1784.
———,	"	November 5, 1786.

Children of Timothy Hatch:

Saluenius,	born	July 11, 1717.
Mary,	"	August 17, 1718.
Jedida,	"	December 30, 1720.
Jethro,	"	September 17, 1722.
Timothy,	"	June 22, 1728.
Deborah,	"	April 10, 1729.
Job,	"	May 10, 1731.

Justus, son of Ichabod Hatch, married Abigail Case, February 15, 1744. Their children were:

Honora,	born	March 16, 1745.
Heman,	"	April 1, 1747.
Darius,	"	September 30, 1748.
Justus,	"	November 1, 1751.
Ruth,	"	January 21, 1759—and two that died in infancy.

Children of David and Anna Hatch:

George,	born	September 29, 1764.
Solomon,	"	November 5, 1766.
Lucy,	"	February 19, 1768.

The descendants of the first Joseph Hatch now in Tolland, are Mrs. Alexander Abbott and her descendants, Miss Ruth Hatch, Frank Hatch and his children, the descendants of Capt. Stephen Griggs, the descendants of Dea. Jabez Kingsbury, and Joseph Tilden and children.

OLIVER YEOMANS was one of the victims at the island of Cuba. He was a son of Elijah Yeomans, and was born in Tolland, November 10, 1740. He was of course about twenty-two years old when he died. There were several families of the name of Yeomans in Tolland at an early date. In 1720 one John Yeomans was selectman; and one John Yeomans, Jr., of Tolland, has a deed recorded, bearing date April 11, 1723. There is no record of his family.

Thomas Yeomans had the births of five of his children recorded in Tolland, viz.:

Thomas,	born	July 9, 1716.
Joseph,	"	March 28, 1719
John,	"	May 10, 1721.
Stephen,	"	July 9, 1723
Ruth,	"	October 28, 1725.

Joseph, son of Thomas Yeomans, married Susanna Richardson, February 1, 1749. They had one child, Stephen, born July 25, 1749.

Stephen, son of Thomas Yeomans, married Jerusha Benton, October 17, 1771. They had one child, Susanna, born August, 1772.

Elisha Yeomans and his wife Mary have the following record:

Jerusha,	born	March 3, 1728.
David,	"	March 30, 1730.
Mary,	"	May 5, 1732.
Jonathan,	"	April 7, 1734.
Hannah,	"	March 8, 1736.

Elisha Yeomans died May 21, 1736.

Elisha Yeomans has this record. Abigail, born February 20, 1735; Elijah, January 17, 1738; Oliver, November 10, 1740; Eunice, July 9, 1746. Elijah Yeomans died March 4, 1750.

Elijah Yeomans, Jr., married Amy Delano, June 17, 1762. Their children were, Abigail, born May 6, 1763; Elisha, November 9, 1764.

Elisha Yeomans married Joanna Baker, June 8, 1769. Their children were: Molly, born March 24, 1770; Anna, August 25, 1772; Elisha, January 27, 1775; Sarah, October 7, 1777.

John Yeomans, Jr., was doubtless originally from Stonington. It does not appear whether those of Tolland bearing the name were his relatives, or whether they came from the same place. But it does appear that the name was in Tolland as early as 1720, and continued in the town until 1777, a period of fifty-seven years, after which the name of Yeomans disappears from our records.

EZRA WALDO was another of the persons who was sacrificed at Havana in 1762. He was doubtless the son of Bethuel Waldo, who moved from Windham to Tolland about the year 1750. Bethuel Waldo was a son of Edward Waldo, who was a son of John Waldo, and grandson of Dea. Cornelius Waldo, who settled in Ipswich, Mass., about the year 1650. John Waldo, son of Cornelius, settled in Windham, Conn., in the year 1698. The records in Tolland do not show the time when, nor the person to whom, Bethuel was married. It commences with a notice of the birth of his son Bethuel, his fourth child, who was born in Tolland, May 23, 1751. Bethuel Waldo, Sen., married Lois Munsell, and had a son Ezra, who was born March 23, 1746. Ezra Waldo was of course but sixteen years old when he enlisted in the expedition in which he died, and was then an inhabitant of Tolland. I can find no other of the name who could have been in that expedition. Bethuel Waldo, Sen., had a son named Henry, born January 10, 1762, who was the father of Lemuel Waldo, now a resident of Tolland, and of Mrs. Frances West, of Coventry. There is a tradition in the family of Henry Waldo, that an elder brother of his perished in the revolutionary army. Bethuel Waldo had an elder brother, named Edward, who was the great grandfather of the writer.

LEONARD GROVER came to Tolland from Coventry in 1756, having a deed of a farm in the north part of Tolland, dated April 23, of that year. He had a daughter born in Tolland, October 9, 1758, and lost two children, one of whom died in 1760; the other May 6, 1762;—after which last date there is no record of him or his family. His name appears on the roll of the company under Lieut. Wills that went to Cuba, with the return that he there died. I am unable to find any further traces of his family.

JONATHAN BURRES or Burroughs was also a victim in the expedition to Cuba in 1762. He came into Tolland about the year 1748; and has a record of the births of six children, to which it is added that he died at Havana, September 7, 1762.

I have stated that JOHN LATHROP was slain by the enemy in the war of the revolution. He was the grandson of John Lathrop, who moved into Tolland about the year 1726, from Falmouth, in Barnstable county, Mass., and who took a deed of a tract of land containing a hundred and twenty acres, bounded east on Willimantic river, which deed is dated June 4, 1726 ; and in which deed he is described as " now resident in Tolland."

HOPE LATHROP, who is reputed to have been the brother of John Lathrop, took a deed bearing date 1726, of Daniel Eaton, of a tract of land in Tolland, containing by estimation one hundred and fifty acres, and is also described as bounding east on the Willimantic. In this deed, Hope Lathrop is described as being of "Falmouth in the county of Barnstable, in his majesty's province of Massachusetts Bay."

There is no record of the marriage of John Lathrop, but I find a record of the births of his children. This is as follows:

David, born October 18, 1723, died October 4, 1787.
Hannah, " July 5, 1725.

Jonathan,	born	September 18, 1727.
Anna,	"	March 10, 1730.
John,	"	May 6, 1732.
Thatcher,	"	January 26, 1734.
Lydia,	"	June 21, 1736.
Elizabeth,	"	April 22, 1740, married Col. Solomon Wills.

John Lathrop, Jr., son of John, married Lucy Gray, of Coventry, December 10, 1754. Their children were:

Susalla,	born	November 23, 1757, married Eliab Ladd.
Presenda,	"	January 30, 1761.
John,	"	April 24, 1763, killed December 10, 1780.
Elizabeth,	"	August 23, 1765.
Elvira,	"	June 13, 1768.
Rowland,	"	March 10, 1771.
Lucy,	"	November 1, 1774.
Jonathan,	"	February 17, 1776.
Molly,	"	September 12, 1779.

ROWLAND LATHROP, the son of John Lathrop, Jr., married Hannah Crafts, of Tolland, January 1, 1799. The following are their children:

Horace,	born	April 23, 1801.
William,	"	January 8, 1806.
John,	"	December 24, 1810, died May 29, 1813.
Benjamin,	"	June 5, 1814.
Mary,	"	July 27, 1817.

Hannah Lathrop deceased October 15, 1820;—Rowland Lathrop married for his second wife, Hannah Cleaveland, of Hartland, Vermont, February 28, 1821. Their children were:

Rollin,	born	December 19, 1821.
Thomas Cleaveland,	"	February 22, 1824.

Rowland Lathrop possessed more than ordinary abilities. When young, he passed for what in those days was called a wild young man, but his wildness ended with youth and he early became a very steady man and a most exemplary Christian. He was a member of the Methodist denomination and was a local preacher. His public performances were creditable for fervency, candor and sincerity. He had a good knowledge of human nature, and had a shrewdness peculiar to himself in his remarks upon almost every topic. Mr. Lathrop was proverbial for integrity and uprightness in all his dealings, and constant and true in his friendships. He was highly esteemed by his acquaintance, and never seemed to be more happy than when doing them some good. He was twice elected to the General Assembly, but never appeared to be over-anxious for political preferment. The influence of his example was most salutary, and a recollection of his guilelessness and simplicity will cause his memory to be long respected. He died September 14, 1844, aged seventy-one years.

ICHABOD, son of Hope Lathrop, Sen., married Abigail Baker, of Barnstable, Mass., November 9, 1732. His family record is as follows:

Abigail,	born	October 15, 1733.
Sarah,	"	March 20, 1735, died June 6, 1739.
Hope,	"	July 6, 1737.
Sarah,	"	January 22, 1740.
Anna,	"	March 26, 1742.
Solomon,	"	May 24, 1746.
Mary,	"	September 14, 1748.

HOPE LATHROP, son of Ichabod, married Hannah Hubbard, of Tolland, May 3, 1760. Their family record is as follows:

Rebecca,	born	October 17, 1760.
Edna,	"	February 15, 1763.
Sarah,	"	July 4, 1765.
Ichabod,	"	June 30, 1767.
Hannah,	"	July 12, 1768.
Second wife:		
Horace,	"	April 25, 1775.
Grace,	"	February 21, 1776.
Solomon,	"	April 21, 1779.
Grant,	"	January 25, 1782.
Sophia,	"	July 2, 1785.
Azel,	"	January 28, 1788.
Laura,	"	November 19, 1790.

Capt. Hope Lathrop died November 8, 1792. He had been four times a member of the General Assembly.

JOSEPH LATHROP married Prudence, daughter of Samuel West, June 17, 1744. They had but one son—Nathaniel, born August 16, 1752, and died April 28, 1771. Daughters: Thankful, born October 21, 1746. Prudence, born August 16, 1749, who died November 30, 1771; and Rebecca, born August 28, 1760. Joseph was a deacon of the church, and nine years a selectman of the town.

John Lathrop married Rachel Ladd, Dec. 20, 1753. Their daughter Rachel was born Oct. 22, 1754.

Melatiah Lathrop married Mercy Hatch, Nov. 15, 1738. Their daughter Deborah was born August 11, 1739.

William Lathrop married Amelia, daughter of Capt. Ammi Paulk, March 22, 1803. Their children were, Kelsey, born October 17, 1803; Julius, born March 17, 1805.

JOHN LATHROP, the first settler, was a selectman two years, and twice a member of the General Assembly. He was one of the first representatives the town ever had, he being chosen with Zebulon West at the Oct. session, 1748. His descendants are yet rather numerous in Tolland.

JOHN LATHROP, who resided in the south-east part of the

town on the farm where his son Charles Lathrop still resides, was not of the above family. He was the son of Zebulon Lathrop, from Lebanon, who received a deed of the above-mentioned farm from Joshua Tilden, March 26, 1800. The ancestors of Zebulon Lathrop were from Norwich. The children of this John Lathrop were:

Justin,	born	September 18, 1802.
John,	"	July 26, 1804.
Charles,	"	December 23, 1806.
Wealthy R.,	"	September 13, 1810.
Samuel M.,	"	August 11, 1815.
Mary Angeline,	"	April 2, 1818.

Amos Cobb, the son of Doct. Samuel Cobb, was killed at the battle of White Plains, Oct. 28, 1776.

Samuel Cobb was born in Wales, in Great Britain, in the year 1716. I am unable to say when he came to this country, and where he was educated. On his tombstone he is described as having been a gentleman of public education, but his *alma mater* is not mentioned. He came to Tolland probably about the year 1743, and took a deed from Robert Parker, of Willington, of a hundred and twenty-five acres of land, in this town, dated Dec. 19, 1744, in which he is described as being of Tolland. He married Mary Hinckley, August 25, 1743, by whom he had two children, Sarah, born July 7, 1744, who married John Slate; and Samuel, Jr., born Aug. 2, 1746.

Doct. Cobb married for second wife, Hannah Bicknell, of Ashford, April 11, 1749. Their children were:

Amos,	born	February 9, 1750, killed at White Plains.
Moses,	"	December 21, 1751, died February 2, 1781, was a physician
Mary,	"	December 29, 1753, married Reuben Chapman first, and Daniel Edgerton second.
Jeduthan,	"	January 24, 1756, married Sarah, daughter of Dea. Elijah Chapman.
Hannah,	"	January 20, 1758, died November 27, 1846, aged 89, unmarried.
Solomon,	"	July 30, 1759, died November 6, 1770.
David,	"	July 6, 1761, married Hope Norris.
Pamela,	"	January 20, 1764, died November 6, 1770.
Daniel,	"	January 21, 1766, married Elizabeth Holbrook.
William,	"	January 20, 1768, married Elvira Stearns.
Ruth,	"	September 29, 1770, married Ephraim West.
Rachel,	"	January 20, 1774, died July 19, 1777.

Samuel Cobb, Jr., married Esther, daughter of Ephraim Grant, Dec. 14, 1769. Their son, Samuel, was born Jan. 30, 1771. He married for second wife, Ann Slate, Dec. 16, 1773. Their children were:

Jeduthan,	born	January 29, 1776.
Amos,	"	January 2, 1778.
Esther,	"	July 4, 1779.
Ruth,	"	February 5, 1781.

Daniel Cobb married Elizabeth Holbrook, May 31, 1787. Their children were:

Achsah,	born	June, 1788.
Horace,	"	November, 1789.
Waite,	"	March, ——.
Betsey,	"	June, ——.
Ruth,	"	April, ——.
Daniel,	"	June, ——.
Luther,	"	——, ——.

William Cobb married Elvira, daughter of Doct. John Stearns, Oct. 29, 1792. Their children were:

Hannah,	born	February 30, 1794.
Alma,	"	September 22, 1795.
Eliza,	"	August 27, 1797.
Elvira,	"	September 15, 1799.
Rachel,	"	December 31, 1800.
Wm. Bicknell,	"	March 9, 1802, died.
Mary Ann,	"	April 2, 1804
Wm. Bicknell,	"	January 16, 1806.
Calvin P.,	"	September 26, 1810.

The descendants of Doct. Cobb, now in Tolland, are: Mr. Levi Edgerton; the children and grandchildren of the late Reuben Edgerton; Mrs. B. L. Young and her children; the children of the late Reuben Chapman; Elijah S. Chapman and his children, all being the descendants of Mary Cobb: Luther Cobb; Mrs. Edmund Joslyn; and Mrs. Dwight Edgerton, the descendants of Daniel Cobb: Mrs. Doctor Ladd; her children and grandchildren; the descendants of William Cobb: and the descendants of Mr. Ephraim West, deceased, who married Ruth Cobb. The descendants of Doct. Cobb are also numerous elsewhere.

Doct. Cobb was one of the most prominent citizens that ever resided in Tolland. He is reported as having stood high in his profession, and as having enjoyed the entire confidence of the community. He was honored by the town and the public with several important and responsible offices. He was eight times elected a member of the General Assembly, and likewise attended two extra sessions. He was thirteen years a justice of the peace when there were but two justices in town; and most of the time was the acting magistrate. In this sphere of duty he gave very general satisfaction, and his ministrations were regarded as equitable, discreet, and promotive. of the public tranquillity. His moral influence in society was very effective in restraining vice and dishonesty, and he did much to encourage sobriety and virtue. While living he was greatly respected, and his memory will long remain as the conscientious, upright citizen, and honest man. He died on the 6th day of April, 1781, aged sixty-five years.

As a branch of the Cobb family, now in Tolland, we can not lose sight of the descendants of Mary Cobb, who became the wife of Capt. Daniel Edgerton. Daniel Edgerton probably moved into Tolland in the spring of the year 1770. On the 20th day of March, of that year, he took a deed of Daniel and John Lathrop, of Norwich, of a part of the farm he afterwards owned in Tolland, and in which deed he is described as being of Norwich. He first married Sarah, daughter of Dea. Ichabod Griggs, Dec. 19, 1771; the record of which describes him as being of Tolland. Their children were:

Sarah, born January 8, 1773.
Phebe, " April 13, 1775.

Mrs. Sarah Edgerton died June 23, 1777. Capt. Edgerton married for his second wife, Mary, daughter of Doct. Samuel Cobb, and widow of Reuben Chapman, Nov. 27, 1777. Their children were:

Daniel, born September 11, 1778.
Reuben, " June 13, 1780.
Sarah, " April 5, 1782.
Mary, " June 27, 1784. died September 27, 1784.
Erastus, " November 8, 1786.
Mary, "
Levi, " December 28, 1791.

Capt. Daniel Edgerton died January 10, 1825. He was very highly respected, and was a very active and useful man. Besides his military rank, he was fourteen years selectman, a large part of which time he was the first selectman and principal manager of the affairs of the town; one year a justice of the peace, (which he probably declined holding longer,) and was chosen a representative to the General Assembly twenty-three times. In stature he was quite six feet high, stout built and well proportioned. In demeanor he resembled a gentleman of the old school,—always dignified, affable, respectful, courteous. He deserved and received the general good will of his entire acquaintance, and discharged all the duties of life conscientiously and satisfactorily, and has left a very honorable and well deserved reputation.

Daniel Edgerton, Jr., married Sarah, daughter of Zebulon Lathrop, May 7, 1801. Their children were:

Marvin,   born January 11, 1802.
Linus,   "   October 4, 1803.
Erastus,   "   June 23, 1806.
Betsey,   "   September 30, 1808.
Phebe,   "   October 23, 1810.

REUBEN EDGERTON married Anna, daughter of Zebulon Lathrop, March 23, 1803. Their children were:

Austin,   born March 26, 1805.
Eliza Ann,   "   September 3, 1807.
William L.,   "   August 30, 1810.
Daniel,   "   September 26, 1813.
Reuben,   "   October 17, 1816.
Lucius,   "   April 19, 1820.
Marvin,   "   December 4, 1828, died December 5, 1829.

LEVI EDGERTON married Edna Grant, daughter of Ebenezer Grant, December 7, 1825. Their children were Sarah Kingsbury, born September 14, 1826, and Amaret Grant, born June 26, 1828.

Capt. Daniel Edgerton, the founder of the above family, had a half brother named Hezekiah, who came from Norwich to Tolland about the year 1770. He was the progenitor of the Edgertons in Coventry, and their descendants. His widow, Freelove, died in Tolland in 1801.

BURYING-GROUNDS.

The first record of any burial in Tolland was made in the year 1735, and is in these words:

"Ebenezer Eaton, a son of William Eaton, died in June the 27th day one thousand seven hundred and sixteen, (1716,) in the nineteenth year of his age, and was the first that was laid in the burying-place of the above said Tolland."

"Daniel Eaton, the son of William Eaton, died July the twentieth day, in the year one thousand seven hundred and sixteen, (July 20, 1716,) in the twenty-third year of his age, and was the second in the burying-place in the above said Tolland."

These young men were the sons of William Eaton, the first of that name in Tolland, of whom I have already spoken. It would seem that the inhabitants of Tolland, by a kind of common consent, set apart a portion of land where these young men were buried, and now included in the south burying-ground, as a public or common place of burial. Whether this was the only spot then used for that purpose, does not distinctly appear, nor does it appear that there was any action of the town or proprietors of the land upon this subject before 1720. At a town meeting held and recorded under date of August 3, 1720, the following vote was passed:

"At a town meeting in Tolland adjourned to the 8th day of the same month it was voted: that there shall be a burying-place where they did formerly bury in, about two acres."

This vote constituted the whole action of the town at that time, and was deemed a sufficient appropriation and consecration of the ground for the purpose of burying the dead. This ground was then common land, and it was permitted to remain in common without being fenced, for about fourteen years. On the 11th day of December, 1734, the town passed the following vote:

" It is further agreed and voted at said meeting *to fence* the Burying-place in Tolland with a decent five rail fence; that is to say—post and rail fence in some convenient time in the year ensuing: Also voted to choose a committee to complete the fencing of the burying-place as aforesaid,—Sergt. Ephraim Grant, Ichabod Hatch are chosen a committee for to do or see said work well done."

In order to have the foregoing vote carried into effect, it became necessary to locate this ground; accordingly a survey was then made by Jonathan Delano, a selectman, and Zebulon West, surveyor, as follows:

" Whereas it was voted by the town of Tolland at a meeting on the 8th of August, 1720, that there should be a burying-place where some dead had before been buried, viz.: about two acres of land, and there being no survey of the same to be found on record: We the subscribers have this first day of March A. D. 1735, surveyed, measured and laid out for the town, two acres of land a little southward of Scungamug pond, containing within the same all the graves that are thereabout; bounding the same as followeth: Beginning at a white oak tree, marked, for the south-east corner—standing in the west line of Doctor James Stimson's land; from thence run with six degrees to the west, twenty-two rods and a half to a stake and heap of stones;—from thence run west twelve degrees to the south, fifteen rods to a stake and heap of stones ;—thence run south, six degrees to the east twenty-two rods and a half to a stake, and heap of stones;—thence a straight line fifteen rods to the first mentioned white oak tree ;—abutting east on said Doctor James Stimson, and west on Daniel Benton ; south on the heirs of Barnabas Hinsdale. The above written recorded March 30, 1735." Signed by Jonathan Delano, selectman, Zebulon West, surveyor.

On the same day Daniel Benton gave a path one rod wide across his land to this burying-place.

On the 16th day of March, 1761, the town passed the following vote :

"Voted to procure two pieces of land of about one acre in each in the northward part of the town for burying-places. Also voted that Timothy Benton, Capt. Isaac Hubbard and Mr. Stephen Steel be a committee to procure such pieces of land by their discretion."

On the fifth day of January, 1762, Timothy Benton gave the town of Tolland a deed of one acre of land for a burying-ground, to be used for that purpose, for the consideration of five pounds, lawful money. This is the burying-ground in the north-west part of the town. Jonathan Ladd, son of Jonathan Ladd, Jr., and Anna his wife, died August 25, 1762, aged two months and ten days, and was the first person laid in this burying-ground. The child was a brother of Eliab Ladd, father of Ariel Ladd, Esq., now of Tolland.

On the seventh of February, 1762, Nathan Flynt, for the consideration of five pounds lawful money, gave the town of Tolland a deed of one acre of land for a burying-ground, which is now the ground in Scungamug village.

With the exception of the north-west, which has been kept in repair by those who felt an interest in its appearance, the town has taken charge of these burying-grounds, has appointed persons to take care of them, (called sextons,) and has done most that has been done to make them even respectable. On the ninth day of April, 1859, the town voted to purchase land to enlarge the south burying-ground, and grade and drain the one at Scungamug. On the thirteenth of April, 1859, the town procured a deed of land lying between the south burying-ground and the highway, which was graded and prepared at the expense of the town, and the town also drained and graded the ground at Scungamug, and erected a substantial stone fence on the side next the road, during the same year.

POST-OFFICE.

BEFORE the year 1795 or 1796, there was no post-office in Tolland. In one of those years an office was established in this town, and Deacon Benoni Shepard was appointed postmaster. Dea. Shepard kept a tavern in the house where Mr. Charles R. Hicks now resides, and kept the office in his house. At that time there was but one mail a week between Hartford and Boston, and that was sometimes carried on horseback, sometimes in a one horse sulkey. No stage coaches passed through Tolland until the year 1807, when a line of stages was established from Hartford to Boston, passing through this town. Within fifteen years after its first establishment, the mail route through Tolland became a great thoroughfare; there was a daily mail both ways, which was carried through Tolland in four horse post-coaches. The route for the mail from New York city to the Eastern States, was through this town, until the western railroad was completed to Springfield, after which the mail was placed upon that route. There was also a tri-weekly mail from Springfield to Norwich, through Tolland, from 1828 to 1851, carried in post-coaches, when it was placed upon the railroad by the way of Palmer. These principal mail routes have been turned from Tolland in consequence of the building of the railroads, so that while other places have been benefited by those improvements, this town has been a sufferer. In place of the mail accommodations with which the town used to be favored, it is now supplied specially with a daily mail from Hartford,—Tolland being the end of the route.

BENONI SHEPARD, the first postmaster, was probably a son of Jonathan Shepard, whose deed of land in Tolland, dated

April 8, 1763, describes him as belonging in Coventry. Benoni Shepard married Desire West, a daughter of Zebulon West, Esq., June 16, 1774, at which date he is described of Tolland. In another record he is found to be of Tolland, May 25, 1772. His first wife, Desire, died July 20, 1778, leaving one child, whose name was Pamela, born January 23, 1777. Mr. Shepard married for his second wife, Anna Alvord, of Bolton, daughter of Saul Alvord, Sen., February 15, 1781. By her he had the following children:

Benoni,	born	January 4, 1782, died August 26, 1799.
Desire,	"	June 29, 1783.
Anna,	"	March 31, 1785.
Sophia,	"	February 3, 1787.
Sally,	"	November 24, 1788.
Lydia,	"	December 14, 1790.
Eunice,	"	March 5, 1794.
Benoni A.,	"	June 28, 1796.
Anson,	"	September 29, 1799.

Mr. Shepard has the reputation of having been a good neighbor, a worthy citizen and a useful man. He was for several years a deacon of the Congregational church in Tolland, and died January 16, 1808, aged sixty-eight years.

Upon the resignation of Mr. Shepard in 1807, Col. Elijah Smith was appointed postmaster, and continued in office until the year 1812, when for political reasons only, he was removed, and Calvin Willey, Esq., appointed in his place.

Col. ELIJAH SMITH was a son of Moses Smith, of East Hartford, and was born January 16, 1767. He was by trade a hatter, and removed to Tolland and set up his business in the Spring of the year 1788. He took a deed of a house and a piece of land in Tolland, from James Wells, dated March 19, 1788. He married Melicent Wills, a daughter of Col. Solomon Wills, October —, 1792;—she died May 22, 1810. He married for his second wife, Lydia Curtis, July 16, 1811. Their children are two sons, born March 22, 1812, whose names are Elijah Wills and Eli Ives;—and two daughters, Lydia Melicent, born August 22, 1817, and Mary Mindwell, born June 4, 1822.

Col. Smith commenced keeping a public house in Tolland soon after his first marriage, at the place now occupied by Ansel S. Barber, and continued in that business until his death,—a period of about fifty years. To say that his house was excellent—that he was a model landlord, and his good lady a princess among landladies—would not be telling the whole story, and would give but a faint impression of the comforts afforded by his mansion. His house was indeed the traveler's home, where a guest had every wish gratified without feeling that some extra effort had been put forth for his special benefit. The Colonel was always cheerful and familiar, without losing any of that dignity so essential to command the respect of others; and without seeming to exercise authority, he always kept his bar-room in such order that one would as soon think he was sitting in a gentleman's parlor as in a place of public resort. The whole establishment was managed upon the plan of having a place for every thing, and every thing in its place; and this general plan had few innovations. At this tavern, Gen. Lafayette, in his tour in this country in 1824, halted and had an interview with some of his comrades in the revolutionary war.

As a citizen, Col. Smith possessed many of those qualities that adorn human nature, and which make a man's society desirable and his life useful. He was once a member of the General Assembly, and as Colonel of the twenty-second regiment was a popular military officer. He was an affectionate husband, an indulgent parent, a kind and accommodating neighbor, and a sincere and constant friend. He was forward in all attempts to build up the interests of the town, active in works of benevolence and charity, and ever ready to relieve the poor and distressed. He took a deep interest in the welfare of young men, often aided them by his counsels, and encouraged them to hope for better prospects when angry storm-clouds seemed ready to dash upon them. The writer has too often experienced his kindness to let his name fade from his recollection so long as his own memory performs its office. Col. Smith departed this life May 24, 1847, aged eighty.

Hon. CALVIN WILLEY was postmaster from 1812 to 1820, when he resigned, and Luther Eaton was appointed in his place. Mr. Willey kept the post-office a part of the time in his own house, being the one now owned by James S. Kent, and a part of the time he had Joseph Howard as assistant, who kept the office at his own residence in the south part of the square roof house near the north end of the village street, now owned by Doct. Jeduthan C. Eaton.

Mr. Willey was born in East Haddam, Conn., September 11, 1776. His early advantages for education were very indifferent, being nothing more than the benefits of the common schools as they then existed. He commenced reading law in the office of the late Hon. John Thompson Peters, afterwards one of the judges of the Supreme Court of Errors, in June, 1795. Mr. Peters was then a resident of Hebron, in Tolland County. Mr. Willey was admitted to the bar in Tolland county, in February, 1798, and first opened an office in Chatham, in the county of Middlesex, but in 1800 he removed to Stafford, in Tolland county, where he resided until the year 1808. While in Stafford he was twice chosen a representative to the General Assembly, and was postmaster in that town from 1806 to 1808, when he removed to Tolland. He was Judge of Probate for the district of Stafford, then including the town of Tolland, from 1818 to 1825—seven years; was six times elected a representative to the General Assembly from Tolland, and twice to the State Senate, upon a general ticket, before the State was districted for the choice of Senators. He was a candidate for the office of Representative in Congress in the year 1821, but was defeated by his own party because he had, in 1820, suffered his name to remain on a union ticket for State Senators, consisting of an equal number of federalists and democrats. Mr. Willey was identified with the democratic party. In 1824 his friends brought him forward for the United States Senate, when the same objection was urged against him. There had always been some rivalry and a little ill feeling between Mr. Willey and some of the prominent politicians in the south part of the county; and hence the strong opposition to Mr. Willey whenever he was a candidate for an office that called for their suffrages. He was defeated as representative to Congress by Hon. Daniel Burrows, a resident of Hebron. In the canvass for the United States Senate in 1824, the citizens in the south part of this county, brought forward as his competitor, the late Governor, John S. Peters, of Hebron. During the session of 1824, Mr. Willey was three times elected by the House of Representatives to the office of United States Senator, by very considerable majorities; and John S. Peters was as many times elected to the same office by the Senate. As the two Houses did not concur, the Assembly adjourned without making a choice. The friends of Mr. Willey were very active in the Spring of 1825 in securing a return of members of the legislature favorable to his election to the senatorship, and succeeded in electing a decided majority in the House of Representatives, which early in the session elected Mr. Willey to that office; but the Senate, as if to try the temper of the House, re-elected on their part Hon. James Lanman, whose term in the U. S. Senate had then expired, and whose place this election was to fill. But the House immediately returned the name of Mr. Willey to the Senate, who upon reconsideration concurred with the House, and Mr. Willey was thus elected Senator of the United States for six years. In this canvass, which had become very animated, Mr. Willey received the support of the remnant of the federal party, which then existed in some strength. They were conscious that much of the opposition to him arose from his conservative course in the election of 1820, and the gentlemen who sympathized with him then, manifested their gratitude by sustaining him for the office of U. S. Senator in 1825. Mr. Willey entered upon and discharged the duties of that appointment, and retired from public life at the close of his term in 1831, and at the age of fifty-five years.

He returned to his profession in 1831, but his absence for so long a time, and the changes in the course of business, had turned the current into other channels, and he was never able to regain the professional standing he enjoyed previous to his election to Congress.

Mr. Willey was a man of more than ordinary intellect, and his attainments as a lawyer were very fair. At one time he stood at the head of the bar in Tolland county. He was devotedly attached to his profession, entertained strong views of the ennobling and elevating effect its practice has upon the mind of the honest practitioner, and maintained that in its benefits to community it stood second to no other. He was very successful before a jury; he always entered into the cause of his client with his whole heart,—indeed, he often became so identified with his client as to make success a matter of personal feeling; and he sometimes lost sight of the true interests of his client in his zeal to defend the claims he set up. At the close of his life, the bar of Tolland county noticed his memory by appropiate resolutions, which by order of the Superior Court were placed upon the Court records.

Mr. Willey was twice married. His first wife was Sally Brainard, of Chatham. They were married October 22, 1798. Their children were as follows:

Sidney Brainard,	born	March 14, 1807.
James Marshall,	"	December 27, 1811.
John Calvin,	"	June 28, 1814.
Sarah Jane,	"	June 29, 1816.
Elizabeth Mary,	"	December 24, 1817.
Asa,	"	September 7, 1819.
George Parsons,	"	July 27, 1821.

Sally Willey, the wife of Hon. Calvin Willey, died February 25, 1827, aged 44. He married Nabby Brainard, sister of his first wife, April 25, 1827. The following are their children:

Harriet Maria,	born	April 28, 1828.
Mary Ann,	"	January 19, 1830.
Lucretia Green,	"	February 4, 1832.
Eliza Hall,	"	May 14, 1833.
Letitia N.	"	February 24, 1835.

Mr. Willey continued to reside in Tolland until the spring of 1854, when he removed to Stafford, where he remained until his decease, August 23, 1858, at the age of eighty-two years.

LUTHER EATON was postmaster from 1820 to 1845, when, upon his resignation, JOSEPH BISHOP was appointed to the office. In the spring of 1850, Mr. Bishop was removed, solely for political causes, and HENRY UNDERWOOD was appointed in his place. Mr. Underwood removed from the town in the spring of 1853, and resigned the office, which in June, 1853, was filled by the appointment of OBADIAH P. WALDO, who held the office until July, 1861, when he was removed, for political causes, and WILLIAM KEITH appointed as his successor.

Thus in sixty-six years there have been but seven post-masters in Tolland, three of whom have been removed from office on account of politics, the others having been permitted to hold the office until it was their pleasure to resign,—one of whom, Luther Eaton, Esq., held the office twenty-five years.

TOWN-CLERKS.

We have seen that a petition was presented to the General Assembly in May, 1716, praying for "the privilege to choose a town-clerk and other town officers," which was negatived. Whether any other petition was ever presented for this object does not appear; but in the year 1717 the town was permitted to choose town officers, and in December of that year commenced the exercise of that privilege. The following are the names of the persons who have been town-clerks of the town of Tolland, with the dates of the commencement and termination of their terms of office.

Joseph Benton, elected Dec., 1717, held the office three years.
Shubael Stearns,   "   1720,   "   two   "
John Huntington,   "   1722,   "   one   "
Shubael Stearns, re-elected, 1723,   "   one   "
Jonathan Delano, elected,   1724,   "   twelve   "
Zebulon West,   "   1736,   "   thirty-four "
Nathaniel West,   "   1770,   "   six   "
Eleazar Steel,   "   1776,   "   nine   "
Benoni Shepard,   "   1785,   "   eighteen   "
Ephraim Grant,   "   1803,   "   four   "
Samuel Ladd,   "   1807,   "   one   "
Daniel Kellogg,   "   1808,   "   two   "
Samuel Ladd,   re-elected 1810,   "   five   "
Eliakim H. Williams, elected 1815,   "   one   "
Luther Eaton,   elected   1816,   "   four   "
Joseph Howard,   "   1820,   "   sixteen   "
Oliver K. Isham,   "   1836,   "   ten   "
Samuel Kent,   "   1846,   "   two   "

William W. Brace, elected 1848, held to April 5, 1852, when Joseph Bishop was appointed by the selectmen upon the resignation of Mr. Brace, and held the office until the annual meeting in 1852.

Gurdon Isham, elected 1852, held the office two years.
Oliver K. Isham, re-elected 1854, " two "
Gurdon Isham, " 1856, and held the office until his death, when Joseph Bishop was appointed by the selectmen for the balance of the year.
Joseph Bishop, elected 1857, held the office three years.
Joseph A. Dresser, " 1860.

I have already spoken of Joseph Benton, and have given such genealogical facts of the Benton family as I had been able to obtain.

SHUBAEL STEARNS, the second town-clerk of Tolland, was one of a family that had much to do in the early settlement of the town. He was one of the grantees in the deed from the committee or trustees, and was also one of the signers of the petition dated May 14, 1716, and May, 1718. He had land allotted to him in June and July, 1720. He was born in Lynn, Mass., August 9, 1683, and married Rebecca Sanford, at Saco, on the 28th day of December, 1704. The following are their children:

Shubael,	born	January 28, 1705.
Rebecca,	"	November 19, 1707.
Peter,	"	August 2, 1710.
Isaac,	"	March 22, 1713.

The record made by Mr. Stearns himself, shows that the children above-named were born before his removal to Tolland. The following were born after his removal into this town:

Elizabeth,	born	August 30, 1715.
Hannah,	"	March 6, 1718.
Sarah,	"	February 29, 1720.
Ebenezer,	"	April 23, 1722.
Mary,	"	April 27, 1724.
Martha,	"	August 18, 1726.

Shubael Stearns was two years a selectman of Tolland.

Shubael Stearns, Jun., the oldest son of Shubael Stearns, Sen., was ten years old when his father removed to Tolland, in 1715. He married Sarah Johnson, of Lexington, March 6, 1726. He remained in Tolland until the year 1754, when he removed from New England.

Between the years 1740 and 1745, the people of New England were electrified by the eloquence of the celebrated Whitefield, whose preaching was mainly instrumental in forwarding the great revival of religion that then spread through the land. The followers of Mr. Whitefield were called *New-lights*, and were not very favorably regarded by the more staid religious community. Their success, however, was so great, that many of the clergy who were then supposed to have permanent livings, were opposed to the revival, fearing that they might be deserted by their hearers, and be compelled to preach to empty seats. Many of them carried their opposition so far as to refuse the revival preachers the use of their pulpits, and actually procured the enactment of a law that under certain limitations confined all preachers to their own parishes,—an opposition as useless as unwise, and only encouraged the very thing it was intended to prevent. The minds of the people, having become excited by the fervor of the new teachings, could not relish the dry, formal services of the settled clergy, which they supposed were conducted by a set of graceless mercenaries, without any of that unction which characterized the performances of the New-lights. The town of Tolland shared the advantages, or disadvantages, of these movements; but the innovators were treated with more favor by the then settled minister, Rev. Stephen Steel, than their associates received from the clergy generally; and the wisdom of the course pursued by Mr. Steel, growing out of his forbearance, catholicity, and kindness, is evidenced by the fact, that in a very few years this sect entirely disappeared from the town, and left him in charge of a respectable congregation without any open dissension.

Among the persons in Tolland who adopted the New-light ideas, no one became so much distinguished as Shubael Stearns, Jr., above named. He united with them about the year 1745, became a preacher, and continued with them about five or six years. In the year 1750 or 1751, he became acquainted with the Baptist denomination; renounced the tenet of infant baptism, and was himself rebaptized by Rev. Wait Palmer, in Tolland, in the year 1751. On the 20th day of May, in the same year, he was ordained to the work of the ministry by Mr. Palmer and Rev Joshua Morse. Several persons in Tolland attached themselves to Rev. Mr. Stearns, among whom were one or two by the name of Paulk. Mr. Stearns and his companions left Tolland in the year 1754, and fixed their residence elsewhere. It does not appear that he started with any particular place in view, upon which to settle. His biographer, from this point, remarks respecting him, that he "resolved to follow the guidance of the spirit, as it should be manifested to him from time to time. The first place at which he made any stay was in Virginia, on Opeckan creek, where there was a Baptist church under the care of the Rev. S. Heton, and where he met with Mr. Daniel Marshall, his brother-in-law, just returned from his mission to the Indian country. Mr. Stearns pitched at a place called Cacapon, not far above Winchester. Remaining there but a short time, and not finding that ministerial success which his impressions had lead him to hope for; he and his company, now joined by Mr. Marshall and his company, removed to North Carolina, and settled at a place called Sandy Creek, and immediately formed a church. He continued to labor with great assiduity, aided by Marshall and Breed. So great was their success, that in a little time this little band swelled to more than six hundred. Mr. Stearns' impressions, respecting a great work in the West, seemed now to be verifying; and considering subsequent events, he must be an infidel who doubts the origin of these impressions.

"He was a preacher of some doctrinal talents, but he was more remarkable for his zealous animating manner. He brought from New England the same tones, gestures, &c., which had distinguished the new lights of that country. He was of small stature, had a very expressive and penetrating eye and a voice singularly hamonious. His enemies, it was said, would sometimes be captivated by his musical voice. Many things are related of the enchanting sound of his voice; and the glance of his eyes which had a meaning in every move. Mr. Stearns continued to discharge his duties as a pastor of Sandy Creek church until a short time before his death, which took place on the 20th day of November, 1771.

He lived and died faithful to the important truths confided to him. Mr. Stearns was an orator of the right sort, and the effects of his public speaking upon his hearers proved it better than if a thousand finished orations had been published from his lips."

It is not known whether any of the family of Shubael Stearns, Sen., remained in Tolland after the year 1754; it is certain, however, that several of them left at that time with Shubael Stearns, Jr., and settled in North Carolina, where their posterity is now very numerous; and where, as has been likewise ascertained, within a few years, the Rev. Mr. Stearns left a very desirable reputation as a pulpit orator.

JOHN STEARNS was a brother of Shubael Stearns, Sen. This fact is verified as well by tradition as by the copy of a deed from Shubael to John, dated Jan. 16, 1720, on the town records, which deed is expressed to be for the consideration of five pounds in money, or its equivalent, in hand, paid by my brother, John Stearns, of Tolland, &c. This deed shows that John Stearns was a resident of Tolland before 1720. He married Elizabeth Barnes, of Tolland, Dec. 2, 1723. The following is their record:

Eleanor,	born	February 13, 1725, died October 2, 1737.
David,	"	December 14. 1725, died February 2, 1725-6.
Elizabeth,	"	May 26, 1728.
Ruth,	"	July 19, 1730.
Lydia,	"	July 25, 1732.
John,	"	January 11, 1736.

Elizabeth, wife of John Stearns, died April 19, 1737. He married Abigail Diggins, of Windsor, April 19, 1739, she died February 13, 1752; he then married Eunice Miller, July 29, 1754. Their children were:

Daniel,	born	January 24, 1756, died April 8, 1756.
Eleanor,	"	August 11. 1757.
Charles,	"	October 19, 1758.
Mary,	"	February 3, 1760, died August 15, 1787.
Sarah,	"	November 6, 1761.

JOHN STEARNS, the son of John and Elizabeth Stearns, was the Doct. Stearns who married a Miss Wills of Tolland, and was the father of Judge Elisha Stearns, of whom I spoke in my lecture on the History of Tolland County. It is only necessary for me to state here that the Stearns family is represented in Tolland by Mrs. Charles R. Hicks and her children; also in Bristol, in this State, by Mrs. Leverett Griggs and Rev. Leverett Griggs' children.

I have before said that Doct. James Stimson married Hannah, sister of John and Shubael Stearns. This relationship is verified by a record of a deed from James Stimson to John Stearns, dated Jan., 10, 1720, in which he sells to "his brother John Stearns of said Tolland." There were of course three families, where one of the united head was a Stearns, among the first settlers of Tolland.

John Huntington, the third town-clerk, has heretofore been described.

JONATHAN DELANO, town-clerk of Tolland, came from Dartmouth, Mass., May 8, 1722. He was a resident of Tolland July 20, 1723, as appears by a deed to him of that date from Stephen Steel. He was twelve years-town clerk, and eleven years a selectman. To judge from his records he possessed a superior English education, and probably was a very useful citizen. His children, thirteen in number, are as follows; the first nine were born in Dartmouth, Mass.:

Sarah,	born	March 18, 1705, married Samuel West, March 30, 1732.
John,	"	December 16, 1706, married Joseph West, May 19, 1725.
Jabez,	"	January 12, 1708.
Nathan,	"	March 1, 1711.
Amy,	"	August 11, 1713, married Christopher West, October 25, 1732.
Jonathan,	"	December 2, 1715.
Barnabas,	"	April 11, 1718.
Sylvanus,	"	May 17, 1720.
Elizabeth,	"	May 15, 1722.
Susanna,	"	June 23, 1724.
Thomas,	"	December 24, 1726.
Timothy,	"	November 4. 1729.
Jethro,	"	October 29, 1732.

JABEZ DELANO, above-named, married Prudence Hobart, of Windham,—had five daughters, but no sons that survived infancy.

NATHAN DELANO married Ruth ———, September 3, 1731, and had three sons: Nathan, born January 5, 1739; John, born December 3, 1731; Jabez, born February 10, 1734, who removed to Coventry, and afterwards to Dover, N. H.

Jonathan Delano married Ann Ladd, October 8, 1754. Their children were:

Jabez,	born	July 1, 1755.
Jonathan,	"	August 10, 1757.
Anne,	"	August 11, 1759.
Philip,	"	June 15, 1761.
Esther,	"	August 13, 1764.
Zebulon,	"	February 19, 1767.
Clarinda,	"	June 10, 1769.

BARNABAS DELANO had one son, Gideon, born November 27, 1742.

Sylvanus Delano married Elizabeth Peck, a widow, daughter of John Abbot, Sen. Their children were:

Sylvanus,	born	April 10, 1745.
Joseph,	"	August 21, 1746, died.
Amos,	"	August 2, 1747.
Sarah,	"	May 28, 1749, died.
Nathaniel,	"	May 27, 1751.
Elizabeth,	"	March 12, 1755, married Solomon Eaton.
Barnabas,	"	May 6, 1753.
Aaron,	"	November 13, 1756.
Anne,	"	April 17, 1760.
Moses,	"	June 15, 1762.

Jonathan Delano was a descendant of Philip De la Noye or De Laynaye, a French Huguenot or Protestant, who to escape persecution in his own country, fled to the puritan brethren at Leyden, and came to Plymouth in the second ship that came to that place, viz.: the Fortune, in November, 1621. From this Philip are descended all bearing the name of Delano in the United States. The descendants of Jonathan are very numerous and respectable, though mostly by female branches. Rev. Stephen West, the celebrated theological writer, was one of them. The representatives of this family now in Tolland, are: the children of Mr Joel West; the children of Mr. Ephraim West, and their descendants; Mr. Luther Eaton and his descendants; Mrs. Anna Johnson and her descendants.

ZEBULON WEST was town-clerk thirty-four years. He was a son of Dea. Francis West, who before the year 1720, was a resident of Stonington. This is verified by the record of a deed from Josiah Rockwell, of Windsor, to Francis West, of Stonington, dated November 29, 1718; also of a deed from Nathaniel Grant, of Tolland, to Francis West, of Stonington, dated March 1, 1720, both conveying land in Tolland. He was a resident in this town in January, 1721, as appears by the record of a deed from John Huntington to "Francis West of Tolland." These records show that he then had over seven hundred acres of land standing in his name, lying principally in the south-east corner of the town. He had several sons whose names appear on the records of the town. Their names are Samuel, Joseph, Amasa, Zebulon, Pelatiah, and Christopher. Joseph and Samuel were in town January 14, 1720, on which day the ear marks of their cattle were recorded. Samuel's mark was a half-penny on the fore side of the right ear; and Joseph's mark was a half penny on the foreside of the left ear.

Samuel West was one of the original grantees in the proprietor's deed, and had land allotted to him with the other proprietors of the town. Francis West took a deed from Nathaniel Taylor, one of the original proprietors, of two lots of land containing one hundred and forty-two acres, " with all rights of division," which entitled him to an interest in common with other proprietors.

SAMUEL, son of Dea. Francis West, married Sarah, daughter of Jonathan Delano, November 4, 1724. The following is their record:

Prudence,	born	September 5, 1726.
Sarah,	"	March 21, 1729.
Samuel,	"	March 30, 1732.
Abigail,	"	July 22, 1734, died February 12, 1750.
Abner,	"	May 1, 1737.
Joanna,	"	December 2, 1739.
Elisha,	"	September 14, 1742.
Anna,	"	September 16, 1745.

Sarah, wife of Samuel West, died November, 1752. He then married Abigail, daughter of Ichabod Lathrop, November 26, 1754. Their children were:

| Ann, | born | September 12, 1756. |
| Ruth, | " | December 21, 1759. |

Samuel, son of Samuel West, married Sarah, daughter of Ichabod Lathrop, March 25, 1756. Their children were:

Sarah,	born	November 19, 1757.
Tryphena,	"	January 21, 1760.
Ichabod,	"	June 7, 1762.
Stephen,	"	February 15, 1765.
Frederick,	"	April 2, 1767.
Grace,	"	September 26, 1769.
Prudence,	"	February 23, 1772.

Abner, son of Samuel West, Sen., married Mary, daughter of Joseph Hatch, 2d, July 3, 1760. Their children were:

Abigail,	born	June 28, 1761.
William,	"	February 12, 1762.
Abner,	"	January 8, 1765.
Mary,	"	March 6, 1767.
Submit,	"	July 24, 1769.

Joseph, son of Dea. Francis West, married Joanna, daughter of Jonathan Delano, May 19, 1725. His children were:

Mercy,	born	April 20, 1726.
Joseph,	"	November 2, 1728.
Joanna,	"	August 21, 1732.
Rufus,	"	October 1, 1735.
Deborah,	"	January 30, 1738.
Bathsheba,	"	July 9, 1741.
Ephraim,	"	December 5, 1747, died September 16, 1760.
Jabez,	"	January 30, 1751.

THE EARLY HISTORY OF TOLLAND. 117

Joseph, son of Joseph and Joanna West, married Lois Strong, March 10, 1752. Their children were:

Joseph,	born	December 21, 1752, died March 20, 1753.
Sarah,	"	April 7, 1754.
Charles,	"	May 4, 1756, died September 18, 1760.
Dorcas,	"	May 17, 1760, died August 15, 1760.
Eunice,	"	December 20, 1762.
Joseph,	"	June 3, 1776.
Salome,	"	February 6, 1769.
Hannah,	"	October 30, 1721.
Zadoc,	"	December 1, 1773.
Joel,	"	March 19, 1777.

This Joseph West was a very useful citizen. He was entrusted with the guardianship of an unusual number of minors, not one of whom was ever known to express dissatisfaction with the management of his property. Towards the close of the revolutionary war, when the financial affairs of the town were necessarily in great confusion, and the state government had required additional duties from towns in their corporate capacity, the people of Tolland elected a board of five selectmen, being two more than the usual number, and Mr. West was placed at its head, though he had, as selectman, long before, gone the customary round of office.

JOEL, son of Joseph and Lois West, married Abina Chapin, of Stafford, October 25, 1798. Their children were:

Lois,	born	February 23, 1800.
Percy,	"	January 1, 1802.
Lester,	"	July 8, 1804.
William,	"	June 3, 1806.
Alden,	"	August 27, 1808.
Chauncey,	"	May 22, 1811.
Elisha,	"	October 22, 1813.
Eli S.,	"	August 15, 1817.
Henry W.,	"	August 28, 1819, who with his family continues to occupy the farm and dwelling-house of his ancestors.

Rufus, son of Joseph and Joanna West, married Sarah Nye, November 22, 1764. Their children were:

Grace,	born	November 1, 1766.
Ephraim,	"	September 30, 1767.
Joel,	"	September 27, 1773, died in infancy.

EPHRAIM, son of Rufus West, married Ruth, youngest daughter of Doct. Samuel Cobb, December 3, 1790. Their children were:

Randa,	born	October 4, 1791.
Rufus,	"	June 30, 1793.
Orson,	"	February 1, 1796.
Carlo,	"	
Bicknell,	"	January 10, 1800.
Sherman,	"	October 20, 1801.
Parmela,	"	September 12, 1803.
Grace,	"	October 29, 1805.
Evaline,	"	June 26, 1807.
Ruth,	"	August 6, 1809.
Ephraim,	"	February 11, 1812, died March 28, 1818.

Mr. Ephraim West died November 2, 1860, aged ninety-three years. Mrs. Ruth West died January 14, 1838, aged sixty-seven.

Amasa, third son of Dea. Francis West, married Amy, daughter of the first Joseph Hatch. Their children were:

Francis,	born	November 1, 1731.
Oliver,	"	October 2, 1733.
Phebe,	"	September 2, 1735.
Lucia,	"	August 9, 1738.
Rebecca,	"	November 26, 1742, died December 10, 1774.
Amy,	"	December 8, 1741, died August 8, 1756.
Mercy,	"	September 16, 1744.
Mehitable,	"	February 7, 1747, died March 24, 1755.
Amasa,	"	May 1, 1749.
Susan,	"	March 8, 1754, died March 25, 1755.

Amasa West married Bathsheba Gibbs, of Sandwich, September 20, 1757.

Levi, born April 27, 1760.

Francis, son of Amasa West, married Abigail Strong, of Coventry, September 13, 1751. He died June 22, 1769. Their children were:

Beulah,	born	September 8, 1752, died April 23, 1755.
Abigail,	"	January 14, 1753, died April 22, 1755.
Dorcas,	"	October 7, 1754.
Amasa,	"	March 7, 1757, died July 31, 1758.
Sarah,	"	August 15, 1758.
Joanna,	"	June 23, 1763.
Francis,	"	May 30, 1765.
Irena,	"	August 9, 1767, died April 15, 1758.

Oliver, son of Amasa West, married Thankful Nye, January 20, 1757. Their children were:

Ebenezer,	born	November 23, 1758.
Anna,	"	July 18, 1759, died July 23, 1765.
Amy,	"	September 9, 1761.
Caleb,	"	July 4, 1764.
Amasa,	"	October 20, 1765.

Zebulon, fourth son of Dea. Francis West, married Mary Delano, of Barnstable, Mass., October 7, 1731. Their children were:

Mary,	born	September 17, 1732.
Stephen,	"	November 2, 1735.
Ann,	"	March 19, 1738, died January 8, 1775.
Thankful,	"	July 14, 1740, died December 15, 1754.
Elijah,	"	April 6, 1743.

Mary, wife of Zebulon West, died July 26, 1743. He married for his second wife, Mrs. Mary Sluman, February 22, 1744. Their children were:

Sarah,	born	January 27, 1745, died October 19, 1750.
Prudence,	"	February 16, 1747, died August 16, 1748.
Nathaniel,	"	September 5, 1748.
Jeremiah,	"	July 20, 1753.
Desire,	"	August 18, 1755.
Sarah,	"	May 27, 1758.

It is probable that Zebulon West came into town with his father, Dea. Francis West, about the year 1720. He was admitted an inhabitant, that is, a voter, September 21, 1725. He was first elected to a public office in the year 1736, and from that time to the day of his death, thirty-four years afterwards, he was always in the possession of some place of public trust; and no man could be found who served in more capacities, or rendered more acceptable service. He was for seventeen years one of the selectmen of the town; he was town-clerk thirty-four years, and a justice of the peace twenty-six. He was the first person ever chosen to represent the town in the General Assembly, and represented the town at forty-three regular sessions; being first chosen in September, 1748, and with one exception was re-elected at every session thereafter until his decease. He was Speaker of the House of Representatives several sessions. He was Judge of Probate for the district of Stafford, from its organization, in May, 1759, to his death. He was also one of the judges of Hartford County Court, several years. All these offices, except those of selectman and speaker, and with the addition of member of the council or upper house, to which he had just been elected, he held at the time of his decease.

Mr. West was rather above medium size—was exceedingly popular with the masses, yet it is said he never associated with them nor was familiar in his carriage towards them. His personal appearance was imposing, and with his deportment, commanded the most profound respect. About twenty-five years ago, a venerable lady, then nearly ninety-five years old, said to me, she had known Zebulon West very well, and had lived near him. She described him as very sedate, inclined to talk but little, but was remarkable for his good temper. When he went into a place of public resort, all present uncovered their heads, and conversation ceased. It should be remarked, however, that in his day respect was mutual,—that the removal of hats in salutation was customary, and that the young were carefully taught to be silent and respectful in the presence of their seniors.

In the petty prosecutions for violation of the moral law,

so frequent in those times, Mr. West carefully distinguished between youthful thoughtlessness and confirmed depravity; and whenever such prosecutions arose from the disposition to annoy or revenge, he took care, as far as possible, to avoid making the law instrumental to gratify private malice under the mask of public virtue. It used to be said that "Zebulon West never did but one wrong thing,"—and that was certainly a very unfortunate one for the harmony of the town. It was the procuring by his superior influence the location of the meeting-house contrary to the just and strenuous wishes of nearly, if not quite a majority of the inhabitants of the town, at a place south of the geographical center. But notwithstanding this momentary resentment, he always exercised an almost unbounded influence in the management of town affairs, and was, through an entire generation, the principal man in Tolland. He educated three sons at Yale College; Stephen, the eldest, was a clergyman, settled in the ministry at Stockbridge, Mass., and became one of the most distinguished theological writers in New England. Nathaniel, the second son, did not study a profession after graduating, but settled in Tolland as a farmer, was elected town-clerk after the death of his father, six years, then emigrated to Vermont. Jeremiah, the youngest son, settled as a physician in Tolland. He was a surgeon in the revolutionary army, was a representative in the General Assembly ten sessions. He was also a member of the convention in 1788, and voted for the adoption of the federal constitution, and he was justice of the quorum or Judge of Tolland County Court fourteen years.

Zebulon West lived upon the farm lately owned by Bilarky Snow, in the south part of Tolland, and died on the 4th day of December, 1770, aged 65.

NOTE.—The record, so far as I have recited it, exhibits the character of Zebulon West as nearly faultless, yet when the whole is seen, he will appear, to some persons at least, in a light that will throw a different shade over this fair picture. Mr. West was a slaveholder and held one of the sable sons of Africa as property. My evidence for this assertion is found in the town's book of records of births, marriages and deaths, from which the following is copied: "Zebulon

West's negro man Bristo, was married to Betty, Molatto woman on ye 21st day of September, A. D. 1757." This record is in the handwriting of Mr. West, and doubtless was made by him when town-clerk.

The name of this man was Bristo Harris, who lived until April 1, 1802, and is still recollected by some of the inhabitants of Tolland.

The darkness of this shade upon the reputation of Mr. West is very much relieved, when we recollect that Connecticut tolerated and protected slavery by its laws, and that our Puritan fathers saw nothing in slaveholding, nor even in the slave-trade itself, inconsistent with the Christian character.

It may here be stated that during the existence of slavery in Connecticut, several families in Tolland were in possession of that species of property, and that on the abolition of slavery by law, several slaves in Tolland gained their freedom. On the occupation of several islands in Narragansett bay by the British, in the revolutionary war, two or three families, with their slaves, came to Tolland and remained here until the enemy were expelled.

Pelatiah, son of Deacon Francis West, married Elizabeth Lathrop, December 5, 1734. Their children were:

Elizabeth,	born	September 17, 1735.
Susanna,	"	March 28, 1737
Eleazar,	"	November 9, 1739.
Hannah,	"	March 28, 1741.
Zerviah,	"	August 2, 1743.
Eunice,	"	April 30, 1745.
Elijah,	"	March 7, 1747.
Daniel,	"	July 22, 1749.
Prudence,	"	June 1, 1751.
Mary,	"	June 28, 1753.

Eleazar, son of Pelatiah West, married Olive Redington, December 6, 1761. Their children; Charles, born October 4, 1763; Thankful, born November 20, 1765.

Christopher, son of Dea. Francis West, married Amy, daughter of Jonathan Delano, October 25, 1732. Their children were:

Priscilla,	born	August 26, 1733.
Francis,	"	October 30, 1735.
Jonathan,	"	December 30, 1737.
Jerusha,	"	April 27, 1740.
Miner,	"	January 9, 1743.
Lois,	"	in Coventry.
Mary,	"	May 25, 1750.

Solomon West, from Lebanon, married Abigail Strong, of Lebanon, October 10, 1743. Their children were:

Solomon,	born	August 23, 1744.
Ruby,	"	August, 1747.
Abigail,	"	December 19, 1748.
Lydia,	"	March 5, 1752, died October 28, 1772.
Esther,	"	March 17, 1754.
Chloe,	"	April 14, 1756.
Stephen,	"	August 19, 1769.
Jerusha,	"	June 6, 1763.

Ensign Solomon West died August 21, 1810; Abigail, his wife, August 12, 1807.

Solomon, son of Solomon West, married Prudence Lathrop, March 22, 1770. Solomon, their son, born July 26, 1770, died August 21, 1771.

Prudence, wife of Solomon West, Jr., died November 30, 1771. His second wife was Catherine Carpenter; they were married February 29, 1776. Their children were:

Jesse,	born	December 25, 1776.
Prudence,	"	April 2. 1778
Sylvia,	"	November 20, 1780.
Ruby,	"	December 19. 1781.
Ebenezer,	"	April 13, 1783.

Solomon West died June 8, 1822, aged seventy-seven years.

John West came from Lebanon: Dorothy, his daughter, born October 1, 1751; Rebecca, born April 7, 1755.

Moses West married Jemima Eaton, August 18, 1751: Dura, born January 23, 1752; Lana, born January 9, 1754; Alice, born September 7, 1757.

The children of Caleb West, whose parentage is not ascertained, are:

Hannah,	born	August 8, 1749.
Caleb,	"	January 22, 1751.
Ira,	"	June 26, 1752.
Jonathan,	"	June 20. 1754.
Roger,	"	Jul. 1, 1755.
Irene,	"	———, died November, 1763.
Susanna,	"	
Priscilla,	"	November 25, 1763.
Kitty,	"	March 20, 1768

Ira, son of Caleb West, married ———, only daughter of Col. Samuel Chapman.

Ephraim Grant, one of the town-clerks of Tolland. I have spoken of in my address on the county organization. I here only trace his genealogy.

NOAH GRANT, of Windsor, was one of the petitioners for a new township, in the year 1713, and was one of the grantees in the first deed to the proprietors of Tolland. He came to Tolland before 1720, and settled on what is now called Grant's Hill. He married Martha Huntington, June 12, 1717. Their children were:

Noah,	born	July 12, 1718, died October 16, 1727.
Adoniram,	"	February 2, 1721
Solomon,	"	January 29, 1723.
Martha,	"	June 9, 1726

One Noah Grant married Susanna, daughter of Jonathan

Delano, November 5, 1746, and had one son, Noah, born June 20, 1748.

Noah Grant, on the first day of January, 1720, deeded a tract of land in Tolland to his brother, Ephraim Grant, of Windsor.

EPHRAIM GRANT married Elizabeth Cady, August 22, 1723. Their children were: Grace, born January 14, 1724; Ephraim, born April 27, 1726.

Elizabeth, wife of Ephraim Grant, died November 8, 1746. He married for his second wife, Esther Ladd, of Coventry, (widow,) September 24, 1747. Their children were:

Eliza,	born	June 25, 1748.
Esther,	"	March 5, 1750.
Eli-ha,	"	March 24, 1752.
Eunice,	"	April 5, 1754.
Ebenezer,	"	August 2, 1756.

Ephraim Grant, Jun., son of Ephraim and Elizabeth Grant, married Mary, daughter of Hon. Zebulon West, December 13, 1748. Their children were:

Ephraim,	born	April 6, 1750. (Town clerk.)
Prudence,	"	September 19, 1752, died October 4, 1760.
Elias,	"	April 7, 1755, died October 2, 1760.
Philip,	"	May 30, 1757, died September 26, 1760.
Solomon,	"	March 21, 1760.
Mary,	"	August 22, 1762.
Ann,	"	January 30, 1765.
Grace,	"	January 16, 1767.
Stephen,	"	March 9, 1770.
William,	"	October 24, 1773
Zebulon,	"	December 9, 1776.

EBENEZER, son of Ephraim and Esther Grant, married Phebe Edgerton for his first wife, April 22, 1779. She died September 29, 1780. She had one child, Oliver, born 1779, died in 1794. He married Juliana Pearce, January 29, 1782. She died December 17, 1783. Ebenezer Grant married for his third wife, Edna, daughter of Hope Lathrop, December 23, 1784. Their children were:

Juliana,	born	November 16, 1784.
Phebe,	"	August 5, 1787.
Harry,	"	July 2, 1789.
Edna,	"	August 1, 1791.
Ebenezer,	"	June 16, 1793.
Oliver,	"	January 31, 1795.

The Grant family is now represented in Tolland by Mrs. Levi Edgerton, George M. Grant, and Edwin Lathrop Grant, with their families. These persons can trace their descent from the first settlers as well by the Lathrops as Grants, they being lineal descendants of Hope Lathrop.

SAMUEL LADD was town-clerk of Tolland six years. He

was a descendant of Jonathan Ladd, who, before 1720, was an inhabitant of Norwich, Conn. Tradition says he first came to Tolland in 1719 ; but it is certain he took a deed of Nathaniel Wallis, of Windham, of three pieces of land, dated February 11, 1720, which lands were situated in Tolland. In this deed he is described as of Norwich, in the county of New London. Jonathan Ladd married Susannah Kingsbury, of Norwich, December 28, 1713. Their children were :

Ezekiel,	born	January 31, 1715.
Elizabeth,	"	March 14, 1716.
Jonathan,	"	March 5, 1718.
Mary,	"	February 6, 1720.
Susanna,	"	February 17, 1722.
Ephraim,	"	January 30, 1725.
Abigail,	"	March 23, 1728.
Zuriah,	"	March 30, 1730.
Jesse,	"	April 10, 1732.
Samuel,	"	March 29, 1734, died December 24, 1736.

Ezekiel, oldest son of Jonathan Ladd, Sen., married Hannah Bigelow, November 3, 1740. Their children were :

Lucy,	born	May 1, 1741.
Samuel,	"	June 7, 1742.
Ruth,	"	January 12, 1744, died September 3, 1766.
Hannah,	"	September 6, 1745.
Daniel,	"	April 9, 1747.
Ephraim,	"	May 11, 1749.
Elizabeth,	"	April 28, 1751.
Elisha,	"	March 7, 1753, died December 26, 1841, at Wilbraham.
Ezekiel,	"	May 1, 1755.
David,	"	July 27, 1757.
Lydia,	"	July 3, 1761.
Eunice,	"	March 13, 1764, died in infancy.

Jonathan Ladd, Jr., married Anna Tyler, June 27, 1751. Their children were :

Anna,	born	August 27, 1752.
Eliab,	"	April 21, 1754.
Ahijah,	"	February 27, 1756.
John,	"	April 3, 1758.
Sarah,	"	April 27, 1760.
Jonathan,	"	June 15, 1762, } twins, died August 21, 1762
Anna,	"	June 15, 1762,
Jonathan,	"	March 20, 1764.
Ruth,	"	March 30, 1767.

Jonathan Ladd, Jr., died August 27, 1810. His wife, Anna, died August 19, 1803.

Eliab Ladd, son of Jonathan Ladd, Jr., married Susalla, daughter of John Lathrop, Jr., January 14, 1779. The following is their record :

Joseph,	born	October 22, 1779, died in infancy.
Luther,	"	December 20, 1780, died in infancy.
Ariel,	"	February 9, 1783.
Stephen,	"	November 8, 1784.
Lura,	"	October 30, 1786, died May 22, 1816.
Roxy,	"	September 8, 1788, died in infancy.
Roxy,	"	January 29, 1790, died in infancy.
Presinda,	"	September 9, 1791.

THE EARLY HISTORY OF TOLLAND. 125

Eliab Ladd died December 15, 1800.

Ahijah, son of Jonathan Ladd, Jr., married Huldah Fuller, of Hebron, February 2, 1785. Their children were:

Lois,	born	November 18, 1785, died May 25, 1787.
Ahijah,	"	February 20, 1787, died June 2, 1787.
Ahijah,	"	August 15, 1788
Levi,	"	December 20, 1790.
Joel,	"	March 8, 1793.
Ezra,	"	February 23, 1795, died February 4, 1810.
Alvan,	"	May 17, 1797.
Huldah,	"	September 26, 1799, in Ellington.
Daniel,	"	June 28, 1804, died February 9, 1807.

Ahijah Ladd died April 15, 1826, aged 70; Huldah, his wife, November 20, 1834, aged 72.

John, son of Jonathan Ladd, Jr., married Esther Wood, of Somers, December 11, 1783. Their children were:

Esther,	born	September 15, 1784.
Luther,	"	May 10, 1786.
Eunice,	"	June 26, 1788.

Also, John, Maria, Laura, Lois, Lathrop and Eliab.

Samuel, son of Ezekiel and grandson of Jonathan Ladd, Sen., married Margaret, daughter of Capt. Samuel Chapman, Sen., April 28, 1768. Their children were:

Ruth,	born	January 18, 1769, in East Windsor.
Samuel,	"	May 11, 1770. Town-clerk.
Margaret,	"	October 8, 1772.
Mary,	"	November 28, 1775.
Wareham,	"	April 23, 1778.
Jacob,	"	December 14, 1781.

Capt. Samuel Ladd died May 18, 1814. His wife, Margaret, died February 4, 1813.

AHIJAH LADD, Jr., son of Ahijah Ladd and grandson of Jonathan Ladd, Sen., married Almy Cobb, daughter of William Cobb, and granddaughter of Doct. Samuel Cobb, January 20, 1818. They had three sons, viz.: William Cobb, born March 26, 1820; Charles Ahijah, born March 12, 1822; and Theodore Stearns, born September 4, 1826.

Mr. Ladd had no opportunity for obtaining an education, other than was afforded by the common schools of his day, but by the closest application to these advantages, he obtained an unusually fair education for practical purposes. He early indicated an aptness for the duties of the sick room; the reputation of his skill as a nurse, probably induced him to study medicine. He accordingly entered the office of Doct. Judah Bliss, with whom he continued until receiving a license to practice in 1813, when he established himself in Tolland, where, with the exception of two years residence in Stafford, he remained until his decease, July 17, 1855, at the age of sixty-seven years.

Doct. Ladd always had a respectable practice; in one or two branches he was decidedly superior; was reasonable in his charges, and very indulgent to his customers. He maintained a respectable position in society, and was a very useful man. He exercised a most wholesome influence in the circle in which he moved; always on the side of good order and strict morality; discountenancing all improprieties and immoral conduct; possessing all the qualities that characterize the good neighbor; and without exhibiting any disposition to complain or wrangle when others were more successful than himself. Conservative in all his actions and modes of thought, he seldom if ever took ultra ground on any subject, and avoided all angry and unprofitable disputations. With a kind heart and honest purposes, seeking to do right himself rather than to compel others to act according to his views and contrary to their own, he secured many friends and was generally esteemed.

SAMUEL KENT is one of the town-clerks who has passed away; I may therefore be indulged in a few words respecting him. He was born in Suffield, Conn., November 27, 1786; was educated as a farmer, and at one period of his life was very successful in the application of his practical knowledge of that business. He occupied a portion of the farm now in the possession of William West, on which he made many substantial improvements. He married Melicent Wills Steel, daughter of Capt. Ashbel Steel, March 3, 1812; and after residing two years in Suffield, commenced mercantile business in Tolland with Doct. Ahijah Ladd; after the discontinuance of which, and in June, 1819, he was appointed Deputy Sheriff for Tolland County, which office he held by successive triennial re-appointments until October, 1835—a period of sixteen years, when he resigned on account of ill-health. He continued to reside in Tolland, (with the exception of a six years residence in Fair Haven, from 1839 to 1845,) where he remained until his decease, May 28, 1854, in the sixty-eighth year of his age.

He was two years selectman of Tolland, and on his re-election the third year, declined to serve longer. He was two years town-clerk, nearly seventeen years deputy sheriff, and nine years county jailer and keeper of the county house. Mr. Kent discharged the duties of these offices with great credit to himself, and to the entire satisfaction of the public. As an executive officer he could not be excelled, and was very rarely equaled. He had great energy, which impelled him to do his duty promptly; and a sympathy which invariably inclined him to leniency towards the poor and unfortunate. Sometimes, indeed, he was far too indulgent for his own interest, and at the commencement of his official life suffered an embarrassing loss by indulgence to an unworthy debtor. But it was one of Mr. Kent's peculiarities to meet misfortunes cheerfully; he never complained so long as he had physical strength to carry the burden; nor did he ever attempt to avoid any responsibility, which either the law or honor cast upon him. He was reasonably successful in business, until his health became so much impaired he was compelled to relinquish the ordinary labors of life. He was attacked with a lameness, ultimately extending to the spine, which continued, sometimes attended with great pain, until his death.

In stature, Mr. Kent was about five feet ten inches in height, rather spare habit; strait and firm in his carriage; quick and active in his movements. He was a kind and obliging neighbor; social and pleasant in his intercourse; honest and upright in his dealings; and ardent and sincere in his personal attachments. He deserved and received the respect and confidence of his acquaintance. He left two children: Elizabeth Sophronia, born September 18, 1817, and James Steel, born July 24, 1819.

GURDON ISHAM is one of the town-clerks whose last record is made. He was the son of James Isham, of Ellington, who moved into Tolland in the Spring of the year 1796. Asher Isham, brother of James, bought a tract of Land in Tolland, of Lathrop Birge, April 10, 1793, which he sold to James Isham, March 1, 1796. James Isham, of Tolland, married

Polly Kingsley, of Lebanon, at Lebanon, April 20, 1796. Their children were:

Oliver Kingsley,	born	March 26, 1797, Physician in Tolland.
Gurdon,	"	December 10, 1800, Town-clerk, died February 7, 1857.
Shubael,	"	February 27, 1804, died July 22, 1825.
Mary,	"	July 15, 1806, married J. Lathrop, died May 2, 1838.

Gurdon Isham was apprenticed to the business of hatting, which he followed through life. He married Abigail Strong, of Columbia, January, 1824. Their children were:

Abigail,	born	November 17, 1824.
Shubael S.,	"	January 16, 1827.
Chester C.,	"	March 18, 1828, died April 4, 1828.
David B.,	"	May 5, 1830.
Abby Jane,	"	April 13, 1833.
Harriet A.,	"	March 19, 1843, died April 7, 1854.

Mr. Isham was captain of the militia company in Tolland when he was but twenty-five years old; was several years county treasurer, and between two and three years town-clerk, which office he held at the time of his death. He united with the Methodist church in 1831; was a most exemplary and useful member during life, entering into the subject of religion with his whole heart, and there are few whose lives are more in conformity with their profession. Honest and conscientious, never seeking popular applause, he was useful in his place; those who knew him best will kindly remember him.

JOHN ABBOTT, of Andover, Essex Co., Mass., removed to Tolland in the year 1720, and purchased the place now owned by James A. Brown, where he lived sixty years. It is said he never failed to attend meeting a single Sabbath until the year of his death, and he usually went on foot. As he was going to meeting one Sunday, he discovered a bear on a chestnut tree, by the side of the road, opposite the house lately occupied by Capt. H. Cogswell, and called out, a bear! a bear! fetch a gun, in a voice that echoed through the forests and was distinctly heard by persons on their way to meeting, a mile north of the meeting-house. A gun was brought and the bear despatched. Persons now living recollect this circumstance. He died November 25, 1789.

This John Abbott had a son John, who married Elizabeth,

daughter of John Stearns, January 21, 1748. John Abbott, Jr., was born September 18, 1725, and died May 17, 1776. Elizabeth, his wife, died January 6, 1783. Their children were:

Nehemiah,	born	December 21, 1748, died August 24, 1751.
John,	"	July 30, 1750.
Nehemiah,	"	August 23, 1752, died September 23, 1776.
Jehiel,	"	June 2, 1755, died April 13, 1776.
Sarah,	"	August 28, 1757.
Abiel,	"	August 16, 1760.
Elizabeth,	"	August 12, 1763.
Erastus,	"	April 5, 176–.
Alexander,	"	April 8, 1771.

John, son of John and Elizabeth Abbott, married Temperance Baker, April 20, 1780. Their children were:

Sally,	born	April 29, 1781.
Polly,	"	March 29, 1784.
John,	"	April 2, 1786.
Elizabeth,	"	October 18, 1788.
Jehiel,	"	September 3, 1795.

John Bliss, Esq., married Sally, daughter of John and Temperance Abbott, May 30, 1809. Their children were:

Sarah Olivia,	born	August 22, 1810.
Mary Eliza,	"	May 21, 1812.
Sylvester,	"	June 29, 1814.
Emeline Eliza,	"	April 11, 1816.

The representatives of the Abbott family now in Tolland, are Doct. Lucius Abbott, Mrs. George Tryon, Mrs. Lucius S. Fuller, and their descendants.

EBENEZER NYE was one of the first settlers of Tolland. He probably came into town before the year 1718, as his name is on the petition to the General Assembly, dated May, 1718, respecting the Coventry lands. There is some evidence tending to show that he came from Dartmouth, Bristol County, Mass. He had land allotted to him in Jan., 1721, Nov., 1722, March, 1723, and at other times. He also purchased lands of others. Some of his land was bounded east on Willimantic river, and is evidently the farm now owned by William Holman, Esq. Ebenezer Nye married Sarah Newcomb, Jan. 13, 1720. Their children were:

Elizabeth,	born	December 14, 1720.
John,	"	November 27, 1722.
Sarah,	"	August 9, 1724, died August 17, 1731.
Ebenezer,	"	May 14, 1726, died February 2, 1727.
Benjamin,	"	May 13, 1728.
Eunice,	"	February 15, 1730.
Lois,	"	May 25, 1732.
Malatiah,	"	April 21, 1734.
Thankful,	"	August 2, 1736.
Samuel,	"	July 20, 1738.
Sylvia,	"	August 21, 1740.

Samuel, son of Ebenezer and Sarah Nye, married Abigail, daughter of Timothy Benton, May 30, 1765. Their children were:

Hezekiah,	born	April 11, 1766, died March 9, 1850.
Samuel,	"	December 26, 1767, died March 23, 1771.
Abigail,	"	May 10, 1770.
Susanna,	"	January 14, 1772.
Samuel,	"	December 25, 1773.
Bathsheba,	"	October 9, 1776.
Joseph,	"	November 2, 1779.

Hezekiah, son of Ebenezer Nye, Jr., married Asenath Buell, Nov. 11, 1784. Their children were:

Abel,	born	January 29, 1785.
Elizur,	"	April 23, 1786.
Jeduthan,	"	February 21, 1788.
Buell,	"	March 7, 1790.
Anne,	"	December 24, 1791, died February 21, 1817.
John Hyde,	"	April 8, 1793.
Marvin,	"	March 26, 1795
Sarah,	"	October 12, 1798, died March 13, 1819.
Austin,	"	March 26, 1800, died June 3, 1817.
Asenath,	"	February 12, 1804.

Asenath, daughter of Hezekiah Nye, married James Sparrow. Their children were, Emeline, born Sept. 11, 1825; George E., born Oct. 22, 1826; John, born March 28, 1834.

Samuel, son of Samuel and Abigail Nye, married Elizabeth Merrick, of Willington, April 24, 1800. Their children were:

Harriet,	born	August 15, 1801.
Horace,	"	August 22, 1803.
Susanna,	"	February 16, 1805, died February 7, 1828.
Anna,	"	August 12, 1810, married William Holman, March 26, 1833.

The Nye family is now represented in Tolland by George Sparrow and his children, descendants of Hezekiah Nye; and by Mrs. William Holman and her children, descendants of Samuel Nye. It is here worthy of notice that the farm, on which Mr. Holman and family now reside, was a portion of the land allotted to Ebenezer Nye in 1721 and 1722, and has, as far as can be ascertained, always been owned by him or his descendants. Ebenezer Nye was a member of the House of Representatives one session, and selectman thirteen years. Hezekiah Nye, his grandson, was a representative three sessions, and a selectman three years.

SAMUEL ABORN, of Lynn, Essex Co., Mass., took a deed of Nathaniel Wallis, dated March 17, 1724, conveying a tract of land in the north part of Tolland, upon the Hockanum, of about ninety-six acres. This tract is the farm lately owned by

THE EARLY HISTORY OF TOLLAND. 131

Parkel Aborn, now owned by Mr. ——— Loveland. I can not ascertain when Samuel Aborn, the first grantee, came into Tolland. The first record of any birth, marriage or death in the family is the record of the marriage of Samuel Aborn, of Tolland, to Mary Ingham, of Hebron, Nov. 7, 1753. The following were their children:

Martha,	born	August 19, 1754.
Samuel,	"	March 23, 1756.
Mary,	"	February 19, 1758, died in infancy.
Mary,	"	July 5, 1759.
John,	"	June 23, 1761.
Dorcas,	"	March 31, 1763.
Elizabeth,	"	May 20, 1765.
Ruth,	"	September 3, 1767.
Reuben,	"	March 5, 1772.

Samuel, son of Samuel and Mary Aborn, married Dorothy Post, of Hebron, Dec. 26, 1782. Their children were:

Samuel,	born	December 8, 1783.
Jedediah,	"	July 12, 1787.
Roxy,	"	October 17, 1791.
Hiram,	"	November 26, 1793.
Dorothy,	"	February 15, 1797, died June 15, 1822.
Mary,	"	October 28, 1798.
Ruth,	"	October 6, 1801.

Samuel Aborn was a veteran revolutionary soldier, that is to say, he was in the continental service not less than three years, in terms of not less than nine months each, which entitled him to a full pension, or ninety-six dollars a year. He died March 11, 1827; his wife Dec. 9, 1834.

John, son of Samuel and Mary Aborn, married Sarah Russell, of Ellington, June 28, 1796. Their children were:

Sally,	born	July 1, 1797.
Laura,	"	January 7, 1799, married Chester Dart.
John G.,	"	July 21, 1800.
Hannah,	"	January 21, 1802, married Alvin Kibbe, 2d.
Dan,	"	October 20, 1803.
Reuben,	"	May 9, 1805.
Lucius,	"	October 13, 1806.
Parkil,	"	June 21, 1809.
Madison,	"	March 28, 1811.
Morton,	"	November 28, 1812.
Maria,	"	married ——— Allen.

John Aborn, died April 19, 1829.

The representatives of the Aborn family, now in Tolland, are Samuel Aborn, Jedediah Aborn and descendants, Parkil Aborn and family, the children and grandchildren of Chester Dart, and Mrs. Alvin Kibbe, 2d, and family.

SAMUEL PAULK was one of the fifty-one grantees in the deed of the first proprietors of the town. His name is not on any of the petitions of the first settlers, but there is a family-record showing that he was one of the earliest inhabitants of Tolland. Samuel Paulk was married to Sarah Slafter, May 5, 1720, and the birth and death of their first child was on the 6th day of Feb., 1721. This purports to be a record of his marriage, "and the birth and death of his child in Tolland," &c. He had other children, viz.:

Mary,	born	February 8, 1723.
Ruth,	"	February 28, 1727.
Noah,	"	October 31, 1729.
Sarah,	"	January 31, 1732.
Abigail,	"	November 15, 1734.
Samuel,	"	April 3, 1737.
John,	"	November 30, 1742.

Widow Sarah Paulk died May 3, 1744.

Samuel Paulk had an allotment of land made to him May 18, 1719, also January 12, 1721. On the 24th day of December, 1722, he conveyed a tract of land situated near Skungamug river, to John Paulk of said Tolland; but I am unable to say whether there was any relationship between Samuel and John Paulk.

John Paulk married Keziah Benton, December 22, 1736. Their children were:

Dinah,	born	April 10, 1738, died March 6, 1747.
John,	"	February 7, 1740.
Lydia,	"	May 22, 1742.
Keziah,	"	October 10, 1744.
Puhamah,	"	January, 1746, died February 10, 1750.
David,	"	March 24, 1749.
Ephraim,	"	December 1, 1751.
Ammi,	"	April 27, 1756.
Jemima,	"	June 28, 1759.

David, son of John and Keziah Paulk, married Margaret, daughter of Ichabod Stimson, February 29, 1776. His children were, Lois, born in Tolland, January 24, 1777, and others born in Vermont, where he removed, but died in Tolland, February 10, 1824.

Ephraim, son of John and Keziah Paulk, married Eunice Harvey, June 25, 1778. Their children were:

Grace,	born	October 31, 1780.
Ephraim,	"	April 12, 1784.
Eliakim,	"	July 27, 1787.
Eunice,	"	February 23, 1790.
Elisha,	"	January 20, 1793.

Eliakim, son of Ephraim and Eunice Paulk, married Sally Craw, December 12, 1816. Their children were:

Laura,	born	January 9, 1818.
George M.,	"	February 8, 1820.
Julius,	"	June 28, 1822, died August 22, 1825.
James,	"	March 19, 1825.
Sarah,	"	March 19, 1827, died July 31, 1827.
Julius A.,	"	August 16, 1828.
Edwin,	"	February 4, 1832, died July 11, 1833.

Ammi, son of Ephraim and Keziah Paulk, married Esther, daughter of Dea. Elijah Chapman and granddaughter of Rev. Stephen Steel, June 6, 1782. Their children were:

Aurelia,	born	December 24, 1782.
Jeduthan,	"	April 18, 1785.
Keziah,	"	September 21, 1786.
Esther,	"	June 12, 1791.
Lydia,	"	February 11, 1794.
Asenath,	"	January 8, 1797, married Oliver Grant.
Ammi,	"	July 1, 1799, died January 15, 1807.
Erastus,	"	May 30, 1802.

Capt. Ammi Paulk was a veteran soldier of the revolution; died March, 1843.

Jeduthan, son of Ammi and Esther Paulk, married Eunice Anna Cogswell, January 23, 1812. His children were Nathan L., born February 12, 1813; George A., born October 27, 1814. Jeduthan Paulk died October 4, 1830.

In connecting the line of the Whiton with the Paulk family, it may be stated that Elijah Whiton, the ancestor of the former family, married Anna Brown, they both being of Ashford, January 3, 1771, and soon removed to Tolland. He took a deed of land of Jonathan Hatch, September 30, 1775, in which he was described as of Tolland. His children were:

Matilda,	born	May 29, 1772.
Martha,	"	February 29, 1775.
Anna,	"	April 6, 1778.
Vodicea,	"	August 9, 1780.
Hannah,	"	January 26, 1783.
Elijah,	"	July 5, 1785, married Keziah Paulk.
Sybil,	"	February 8, 1788, died February 28, 1790.
Maria,	"	October 16, 1790.
Stephen,	"	April 7, 1794.

Elijah Whiton, Sen., died May 5, 1804.

Elijah, son of Elijah and Anna Whiton, married Keziah, daughter of Capt. Ammi Paulk, March 23, 1808. Their children were:

Ammi,	born	April 3, 1809, died July 7, 1836.
Maria,	"	May 19, 1811, married D. Mathewson and died.
Elijah,	"	March 4, 1813.
Luther,	"	January 20, 1816.
Calvin,	"	February 18, 1818.
Stephen,	"	March 19, 1820.
Marcia,	"	May 14, 1822, died February 11, 1824.
Erastus,	"	May 18, 1824.

Jonathan Paulk, who accompanied Shubael Stearns to North Carolina, had the following children recorded in Tolland:

Esther,	born	November 7, 1731.
Micajah	"	October 7, 1733.
Ruth,	"	March 18, 1736.
Zechariah,	"	March 4, 1738, died in infancy.

The representatives of the Paulk family, now in Tolland, are Miss Eunice Paulk, Mrs. Joseph A. Dresser and child, Messrs. Calvin and Stephen Whiton, 2d, and their children, and Messrs. George M. and Edwin L. Grant, with their children.

The name of LOOMIS is often found upon the early records of the town. Enoch Loomis, Moses Loomis and Joshua Loomis are all grantees in the deed to the first proprietors. They were evidently residents of Windsor. Joshua Loomis signed the petitions of May, 1716, and May, 1718. Land was allotted to him in March and June, 1721. Hezekiah Loomis received an allotment of land, September, 1720, and June, 1721. He was a resident of Windsor in July, 1720, but was a resident of Tolland June 12, 1724.

Solomon Loomis, of Windsor, received a conveyance of land in Tolland from Samuel Cook, of Tolland, June 1, 1724. Solomon Loomis married Abigail Strong, of Windsor, June 28, 1727. Their children were:

Abigail,	born	April 18, 1728.
Solomon,	"	November 4, 1732.
Anna,	"	March 29, 1735.
Esther,	"	July 8, 1738, died June 17, 1751.

Solomon, son of Solomon and Abigail Loomis, married Mary, daughter of Capt. Samuel Chapman. Their children were:

Simon,	born	March 7, 1758.
Solomon,	"	September 27, 1760.
Luke,	"	April 11, 1764, died in infancy.
Nathaniel,	"	January 5, 1766.
Epaphras,	"	September 20, 1768.

Mary, wife of Solomon Loomis, died February 11, 1774, aged forty-two. Solomon Loomis married for his second wife, Mary Johnson, of Stafford, December 21, 1775. Their children were:

Jeduthan,	born	November 10, 1777.
Elisha,	"	January 27, 1779.
Mary,	"	November 5, 1780.
Justin,	"	July 10, 1783.
Ralph,	"	February 28, 1785.
Ruth,	"	April 11, 1787.

Epaphras, son of Solomon and Mary Loomis, married Abigail Grover, Nov. 27, 1794. Their children were:

Almon,	born	October 3, 1804, died March 6, 1818.
Elmer,	"	February 7, 1810.

Elmer Loomis lived and died on the farm of his ancestors,

now owned by Doct. Eaton, leaving three children, viz.: Mary Chapman, born Dec. 7, 1833; Caroline, born March 13, 1835; and Frances Eliza, born May 30, 1837.

Joshua Loomis married Deborah Elmer, of Windsor, April 6, 1737. Their children were:

Priscilla,	born	August 6, 1749.
Joshua,	"	January 12, 1751.
Eleazer,	"	May 26, 1752.
Deborah,	"	August 5, 1754.
Mary,	"	June 26, 1756.

Eleazar Loomis married Jemima Crandall, Sept. 8, 1774. Their children were:

Samuel,	born	September 27, 1775.
Grace,	"	October 17, 1777.
Ashbel,	"	September 16, 1779.
Esther,	"	September 14, 1781.

Hezekiah Loomis married Hepzibah Thacher, Nov. 14, 1724. Their children were:

Hepzibah,	born	January 1, 1725.
Hezekiah,	"	August 11, 1728.
Elizabeth,	"	August 8, 1731.
Ebenezer,	"	November 22, 1734, probably died young.
Mary,	"	July 13, 1737.
Nathaniel,	"	October 8, 1740.
Ebenezer,	"	October 15, 1743.

Simon Loomis married Molly Carpenter, March 8, 1787. Their children were, Luther, born April 10, 1787; Nathaniel, born April 30, 1790; Sally, born June 6, 1792.

Elisha Loomis married Eunice Hatch, July 1[?], 1802. Their children were:

Alanson,	born	October 3, 1803.
Minerva,	"	September 15, 1805.
Jeduthan,	"	November 17, 1807.
Hannah,	"	June 18, 1810.

CENSUS OF TOLLAND.

The first census of Tolland I can find, was taken in the year 1756, when the number of inhabitants was found to be nine hundred and seventeen. The last census was taken in 1860, after a lapse of one hundred and four years, during which time the town had gained three hundred and ninety-three.

Second census, 1774 Whole No., 1262—gain in 14 years, 345
Third   "   1790   "   1538   " 16 " 276
Fourth   "   1800   "   1638   " 10 " 100
Fifth   "   1810   "   1610—loss in 10 "   28
Sixth   "   1820   "   1607   " 10 "   3
Seventh "   1830   "   1698—gain in 10 "   91
Eighth   "   1840   "   1556—loss in 10 " 142
Ninth   "   1850   "   1406   " 10 " 150
Tenth   "   1860   "   1310   " 10 "   96

There are other topics connected with the history of Tolland that should have been noticed; such as the exertions of the first settlers relative to public or common school education; changes in style of living and architecture; improvements in learning, in husbandry, and in various other matters; but time forbids, and I must leave them to other pens. In concluding my present labor, it is proper briefly to remark, that the leading idea which seemed to control the acts of the first settlers of Tolland, was the establishment and support of institutions for public worship. To this one point their hopes centered, and their entire energies were directed. Next to this, they regarded the maintenance of the government under which they lived, as a conscientious duty;—hence their readiness at all times to volunteer on hazardous service, not only in the colonial wars, but in others in which the parent country was engaged. They never harbored a thought of disloyalty until the hand of tyranny fell upon a city in a neighboring colony, when their sympathies for the oppressed were immediately aroused. They then entered into the defense of their inalienable rights with the same earnestness that characterized their devotion to the religion they professed, and pursued it with the same unanimity and unconquerable persistency. I have never heard that there was a single tory in Tolland during the whole of the revolutionary war.

They were also an united people, remarkable for their stability of character and freedom from schism and discontent. This is evidenced by the tenure by which all offices, civil, military, and ecclesiastical, were held. These offices were regarded as having been instituted for the benefit of society rather than as rewards for partisan services; and the question was—who *can* render the best service to society? instead of —who *has* best served his party. They were also essentially a moral as well as a religious people. To do right, was the ruling motive of that age; and to know the right was the great object of their lives. Their labors have ceased and they have gone to their reward. Some of us are now occupying their places; busying ourselves in the same pursuits; animated by the same hopes; depressed by the same fears, and forgetting that our labors, like theirs, must soon end. Some of us have passed the meridian of life, and are now in the front rank; with no shield to ward off the arrow of the relentless destroyer: and although we do not present a shining mark for death's unerring aim—yet we can not be unconscious that the frosts of age are chilling the aspirations of youth, and closing around us the curtain that will shut us out from the scenes of earth. In the light of this thought, how important is the question, Is our work done, and well done? Is there nothing more we can do to make life more desirable, and the world better and happier? Are we prepared to put off the armor and leave the field? If so, ours is a happy condition; and the consciousness that we have done our whole duty will lighten the darkness of the future, and render our pathway to the tomb peaceful and blessed. But if any thing remains to be done, let us improve the present moment to accomplish it; nor let our efforts cease until the great work of life is ended, and the Master calls for us to participate in the employments of the happy spirit land.

MEMBERS OF THE HOUSE OF REPRESENTATIVES.

It was not the policy of the Colony to impose any taxes upon new towns constituted by the General Court, until they had acquired stability and wealth, and those towns were never represented in the General Court until they were required to pay taxes to the treasury of the Colony. But so inseparable were taxation and representation connected in the minds of our forefathers, that just as soon as the government imposed a tax upon a town, their representatives would immediately be sent to the General Court. The following is the first act of the General Court requiring the town of Tolland to pay taxes, and was passed May Session, 1747. "Resolved by this Assembly, that the town of Tolland send into this assembly in October next the sum total of their List as the law directs." The town sent to the General Court in October, 1747, the sum total of its list, amounting to the sum of £7478, 19s. 0d., equal to $24,929.83. A tax of two pence on the pound was laid on this list at the October Session, 1747, and at the next October Session the town was first represented in the General Court. The following is a list of the representatives in the General Assembly, from October, 1748, to May, 1861, inclusive:

1748	Oct.,	Zebulon West, John Lathrop.	1754	Oct.,	Samuel Cobb.
1749	May,	Same.	1755	Mch.,	Same.
	Oct.,	Zebulon West, Joshua Wills.		May,	Samuel Chapman, Ishabod Hinckley.
1750	May,	Zebulon West, John Lathrop.		Aug.,	Same.
				Oct.,	Zebulon West, Samuel Chapman.
	Oct.,	Same.	1756	Jan.,	Same.
1751	May,	Same.		Mar.,	Same.
	Oct.,	Zebulon West, Joshua Wills.		May,	Zebulon West.
				Sept.,	Zebulon West.
1752	May,	Same.		Oct.,	Zebulon West, Samuel Chapman.
	Oct.,	Same.			
1753	May,	Ebenezer Nye, Zebulon West.	1757	Jan.,	Same.
				Feb.,	Samuel Chapman.
	Oct.,	Zebulon West, Joshua Wills.		May,	Zebulon West, Joshua Wills.
1754	May,	Same.		Oct.,	Zebulon West, Samuel Chapman.
	Oct.,	Zebulon West,			

THE EARLY HISTORY OF TOLLAND.

1758	Mch.	Same.
	May,	Zebulon West, Samuel Cobb.
	Oct.,	Zebulon West, Joshua Wills.
1759	Feb.,	Same.
	Mch.,	Same.
	May,	Same.
	Oct.,	Same.
1760	Mch.,	Same.
	May,	Same.
	Oct.,	Same.
1761	Mch.,	Same.
	May,	Zebulon West, Elisha Steel.
	Oct.,	Same.
1762	Mch.,	Same.
	May,	Zebulon West, Samuel Chapman.
	Oct.,	Same.
1763	May,	Same.
	Oct.,	Zebulon West, Joshua Wills.
1764	Mch.,	Same.
	May,	Zebulon West, Samuel Chapman.
	Oct.,	Same.
1765	May,	Same.
	Oct.,	Zebulon West, Elijah Chapman.
1766	May,	Zebulon West, Samuel Chapman.
	Oct.,	Same.
1767	Jan.,	Same.
	May,	Same.
	Oct.,	Same.
1768	May,	Zebulon West, Samuel Cobb.
	Oct.,	Zebulon West, Samuel Chapman.
1769	Jan.,	Same.
	May,	Same.
	Oct.,	Same.
1770	May,	Same.
	Oct.,	Samuel Chapman, Samuel Cobb.
1771	May,	Same.
	Oct.,	Same.
1772	May,	Same.
	Oct.,	Samuel Chapman, Elisha Steel.
1773	May,	Same.
	Oct.,	Samuel Chapman, Ichabod Griggs.
1774	Jan.,	Same.
	May,	Samuel Chapman, Samuel Cobb.
1774	Oct.,	Samuel Cobb, Eleazar Steel.
1775	Mch.,	Same.
	May,	Solomon Wills, Samuel Chapman.
	Oct.,	Ichabod Griggs, James Chamberlain.
	Dec.,	Same.
1776	May,	Samuel Chapman, Solomon Wills.
	June,	No names recorded.
	Oct.,	Ichabod Griggs, Elijah Chapman.
	Nov.,	Same.
	Dec.,	Same.
1777	May,	Samuel Chapman, Solomon Wills.
	Aug.,	No names recorded.
	Oct.,	Samuel Chapman, Ichabod Griggs.
1778	Jan.,	Same.
	Feb.,	Same.
	May,	Solomon Wills, Samuel Chapman.
	Oct.,	Same.
1779	Jan.,	Same.
	April,	No names recorded.
	May,	Same.
	Oct.,	Elijah Robinson, Samuel Cobb.
1780	Jan.,	Same.
	April,	Same.
	May,	Samuel Chapman, Hope Lathrop.
	Oct.,	Same.
	Nov.,	Same.
1781	Feb.,	Same.
	May,	Solomon Wills, Hope Lathrop.
	Oct.,	Hope Lathrop, Elijah Chapman.
1782	Jan.,	Same.
	May,	Elijah Chapman, Solomon Wills.
1782	Oct.,	Solomon Wills, Elijah Chapman.
1783	Jan.,	No names recorded.
	May,	Samuel Chapman, Solomon Wills.
	Oct.,	Solomon Wills, Eleazar Steel.
1784	Jan.,	Same.
	May,	Samuel Chapman, Solomon Wills.
1784	Oct.,	Solomon Wills, Ichabod Hinckley.
1785	May,	Same.

1785	Oct.,	Solomon Wills,	1802	May,	Same.
		Jeremiah West.		Oct.,	Same.
1786	May,	Jeremiah West,	1803	May,	Same.
		Samuel Ladd.		Oct.,	Same
	Oct.,	Solomon Wills,	1804	May,	Samuel Whittlesey,
		Samuel Chapman.			Jeremiah West.
1787	May,	Same.		Oct.,	Jeremiah West,
	Oct.,	Samuel Chapman.			Jonathan Barnes.
Convention,			1805	May,	Samuel Whittlesey,
1788	Jan.,	Samuel Chapman.			Samuel Ladd.
		Jeremiah West.		Oct.,	Jonathan Barnes,
1788	May,	Samuel Chapman,			Daniel Edgerton.
		Jeremiah West.	1806	May,	Same.
	Oct.,	Solomon Wills,		Oct.,	Same.
		Samuel Chapman.	1807	May,	Jeduthan Cobb,
1789	Jan.,	Same.			Samuel Ladd.
	May,	Same.		Oct.,	Jonathan Barnes,
	Oct.,	Same.			Jabez Kingsbury.
1790	May,	Jeremiah West,	1808	May,	Jeduthan Cobb,
		Solomon Wills.			Ashbel Chapman.
	Oct.,	Solomon Wills,		Oct.,	Same.
		Samuel Ladd.	1809	May,	Jonathan Barnes,
	Dec.,	Same.			Jabez Kingsbury.
1791	May,	Jeremiah West,		Oct.,	Same.
		Solomon Wills.	1810	May,	Jonathan Barnes,
	Oct.,	Same.			Samuel Ladd.
1792	May,	Jeremiah West,		Oct.,	Samuel Ladd,
		Samuel Ladd.			Calvin Willey.
	Oct.,	Same.	1811	May,	Calvin Willey,
1793	May,	Same.			Ashbel Chapman.
	Oct.,	Jeremiah West,		Oct.,	Calvin Willey,
		Daniel Edgerton.			Ezra Chapman.
1794	May,	Same.	1812	May,	Ashbel Chapman,
	Oct.,	Daniel Edgerton,			Calvin Willey.
		Elijah Chapman, Jr.		Aug.,	Same
1795	May,	Daniel Edgerton,		Oct.,	Jonathan Barnes,
		Samuel Ladd.			Elisha Stearns.
	Oct.,	Same.	1813	May,	Same.
1796	May,	Same.		Oct.,	Same.
	Oct.,	Daniel Edgerton,	1814	May,	Same.
		Solomon Wills.		Oct.,	Eliakim Chapman,
1797	May,	Daniel Edgerton,			Elisha Stearns.
		Samuel Ladd.	1815	Jan.,	Same.
	Oct.,	Daniel Edgerton,		May,	Jonathan Barnes,
		Elijah Chapman, Jr.			Elisha Stearns.
1798	May,	Daniel Edgerton,		Oct.,	Ephraim West,
		Samuel Ladd.			Elijah Smith.
	Oct.,	Jeremiah West,	1816	May,	Jonathan Barnes,
		Jonathan Barnes.			Ephraim West.
1799	May,	Daniel Edgerton,		Oct.,	Eliphalet Young,
		Jonathan Barnes.			Jonathan Barnes.
	Oct.,	Same.	1817	May,	Same.
1800	May,	Jonathan Barnes,		Oct.,	Same.
		Daniel Edgerton.	1818	May,	Eliphalet Young,
	Oct.,	Same.			Gurdon Thompson.
1801	May,	Same.	Convention,		
	Oct.,	Same.	1818	Aug.,	Eliphalet Young,

THE EARLY HISTORY OF TOLLAND.

1818	Aug.,	Ashbel Chapman.	1839	Elisha Stearns.
	Oct.,	Eliphalet Young,	1840	Ariel Ladd,
		William Eldredge.		Seth D. Griggs.
1819		William Eldredge,	1841	Ebenezer West,
		Hezekiah Nye.		Oliver Lord.
1820		Calvin Willey,	1842	Wm. C. Newcomb,
		Ashbel Chapman.		Luther C. Anderson.
1821		Calvin Willey,	1843	Same.
		Hezekiah Nye.	1844	Talmon Cross,
1822		Hezekiah Nye,		Benjamin L. Young.
		Ezra Chapman.	1845	Same.
1823		Eliphalet Young,	1846	Obadiah P. Waldo,
		George M. Hyde.		John P. Brigham.
1824		George M. Hyde,	1847	Loren P. Waldo,
		Cordial Newcomb.		William W. Eaton.
1825		Jeremiah Parish,	1848	Same.
		George M. Hyde.	1849	Joseph Clark,
1826		Cordial Newcomb,		Oliver K. Isham.
		Jeremiah Parish.	1850	Ashbel Chapman,
1827		Same.		Chauncey Griggs.
1828		Elisha Stearns,	1851	Sherman Chapman,
		Jeremiah Parish.		Ira K. Marvin.
1829		George M. Hyde,	1852	William Holman,
		Rowland Lathrop.		Benjamin Fuller.
1830		Eli Baker,	1853	Joseph A. Strait,
		Rowland Lathrop.		Orrin Ward.
1831		Eli Baker,	1854	Alvin P. Hyde,
		George M. Hyde.		Lucius S. Fuller.
1832		Loren P. Waldo,	1855	Benjamin D. Benton,
		Eli Baker.		Aner Grover.
1833		Loren P. Waldo,	1856	William Clark, 2d.,
		Novatus Chapman.		Daniel Grover, 2d.
1834		Loren P. Waldo,	1857	Joseph Clark,
		Eli Baker.		Joshua Griggs.
1835		Novatus Chapman,	1858	Alvin P. Hyde,
		Cordial Newcomb.		Elijah Ashley.
1836		Carlos Chapman,	1859	Charles Lathrop,
		John Warren.		Alvin Kibbe, 2d.
	Dec.,	Same.	1860	William C. Ladd,
1837		Same.		Orson A. Richardson.
1838		Elisha Stearns,	1861	Joseph Bishop,
		Chauncey Griggs.		Jabez West.
1839		Loren P. Waldo,	Oct.,	Same.

JUSTICES OF THE PEACE.

By the provisions of the act of the General Assembly, passed in 1711, justices of the peace were to be appointed by the General Assembly, annually, and commissioned by the

THE EARLY HISTORY OF TOLLAND.

Governor for the time being, under the seal of the State. This provision was adopted in the constitution in 1818, but was changed by an amendment adopted in 1850, by which justices of the peace are to be appointed by the electors of the several towns. The statute of 1851 provides that they shall be appointed for two years.

The following is a list of the justices of the peace in the town of Tolland from the first settlement to 1861 :

Josiah Goodrich, from	1727 to 1733	
John Huntington, "	1733 to 1737	
Samuel Chapman, "	1737 to 1745	
Zebulon West, "	1745 to 1770	
John Lathrop, "	1752 to 1753	
Elisha Steel, "	1761 to 1766	
Samuel Cobb, "	1768 to 1780	
Samuel Chapman, "	1772 to 1797	
Solomon Wills, "	1781 to 1785	
Jeremiah West, "	1786 to 1794	
Samuel Whittlesey, "	1795 to 1805	
Daniel Edgerton, "	1798 to 1799	
Jonathan Barnes, "	1798 to 1811	
also, "	1813 to 1829	
Jabez Kingsbury, "	1806 to 1817	
Elisha Stearns, "	1806 to 1819	
also, "	1828 to 1833	
also, "	1834 to 1845	
Daniel Kellogg, "	1811 to 1813	
John Bliss, "	1811 to 1818	
Judah Bliss, "	1812 to 1814	
Solomon L. Fuller, "	1813 to 1817	
Calvin Willey, "	1818 to 1845	
Ashbel Chapman, "	1818 to 1823	
Eliphalet Young, "	1820 to 1836	
Jeremiah Parish, "	1821 to 1845	
George M. Hyde, "	1824 to 1841	
Loren P. Waldo, "	1830 to 1853	
John Warren, "	1830 to 1836	
also, "	1842 to 1844	
also, "	1851 to 1854	
Carlos Chapman, "	1830 to 1833	
Ezra Chapman, "	1833 to 1837	
also, "	1841 to 1846	
Oliver Lord, "	1837 to 1842	
Novatus Chapman, "	1836 to 1840	
Talmon Cross, "	1836 to 1840	
also, "	1842 to 1850	
Ariel Ladd, "	1838 to 1840	
also, "	1842 to 1850	
Warren Fitch, "	1838 to 1843	
Seth D. Griggs, "	1838 to 1841	
Stephen Ladd, "	1841 to 1843	
Ebenezer West, "	1840 to 1849	
Jedut'n Gleason, from	1840 to 1841	
Zalmon A. Storrs, "	1841 to 1853	
Ashbel Chapman, "	1842 to 1847	
also, "	1851 to 1857	
Sherm'n Chapman, "	1842 to 1847	
also, "	1856	
Obadiah P. Waldo, "	1842 to 1844	
also, "	1849 to 1851	
also, "	1852 to 1854	
Wyllys Gilbert, "	1844 to 1845	
Daniel Grover, "	1844 to 1846	
Jonathan R. Flynt, "	1845 to 1846	
Luth. C. Anderson, "	1846 to 1856	
Asa Willey, "	1846 to 1847	
Gurdon Isham, "	1846 to 1847	
Ralph R. Griggs, "	1846 to 1847	
also, "	1854 to 1858	
John S. Lyon, "	1846 to 1847	
John W. Gager, "	1847 to 1850	
Chauncey Griggs, "	1847	
Sidney Stanley, "	1847 to 1851	
William W. Eaton, "	1848 to 1850	
Sam'l D. Merrick, "	1848 to 1851	
Calvin Whiton, "	1848 to 1850	
John Lyon, "	1849 to 1850	
Hen'y Underwood, "	1849 to 1850	
Alfred Young, "	1849 to 1853	
Alvan P. Hyde, "	1850	
Benjamin Fuller, "	1850 to 1851	
Myron L. Mason, "	1851 to 1852	
George Eaton, "	1852 to 1858	
Joseph Bishop, "	1854	
Wm. L. Edgerton, "	1854 to 1858	
Geo. H. Kingsbury, "	1854	
Jere. S. Parish, "	1854 to 1855	
William Sumner, "	1854 to 1856	
Geo. D. Hastings, "	1856	
Henry W. West, "	1856	
Edwin E. Mirvin, "	1858 to 1860	
Nathan Pierson, "	1858	
Orrin Ward, "	1858	
James A. Brown, "	1860	
Elij'h S. Chapman, "	1860	
Porter Walbridge, "	1860	

SELECTMEN.

Towns were authorized by the act of 1672 " to choose a convenient number not exceeding seven of their inhabitants, able, discreet and of good conversation, to be selectmen or townsmen, to take care of and order the prudential affairs of their town." By the constitution of the State adopted in 1818, it is made " the duty of each town to elect annually selectmen and such officers of local police as the laws may prescribe."

By the provision of the statutes of 1821, towns were annually to choose and appoint a convenient number, not exceeding seven, to be selectmen, and by the statute of 1852 they are to be chosen by ballot.

The first selectmen chosen in the town of Tolland were chosen in the year 1717. The following named persons have held the office of selectmen in the town of Tolland, during the year prefixed to the names of each respectively:

1717 William Eaton, Jonathan Willis, Daniel Benton.
1718 "   "   Nathaniel Taylor.
1719 "   Joseph Benton,   "
1720 John Yeomans, Francis West, Ebenezer Nye, John Stiles, Daniel Benton.
1721 Daniel Eaton, Joseph Hatch, Joseph Park, Shubael Stearns, John Stiles.
1722 Francis West, John Huntington, Noah Grant.
1723 Daniel Eaton, Shubael Stearns, Peter Emmons.
1724 Jonathan Delano, Samuel Benton, Noah Grant.
1725 "   "   "
1726 Hope Lathrop, Jonathan Delano, Peter Emmons.
1727 Josiah Goodrich, Hope Lathrop, Peter Emmons, Samuel Benton, Jonathan Delano.
1728 Jonathan Delano, Josiah Goodrich, Samuel Benton, Joseph Baker.
1729 No record to be found.
1730 Josiah Goodrich, Jonathan Delano, Ebenezer Nye.
1731 Jonathan Delano, Ebenezer Nye, Samuel Chapman.
1732 "   James Chapman, Ebenezer Nye.
1733 "   Ebenezer Nye, Samuel Chapman.
1734 "   Ichabod Hinckley,   "
1735 "   Samuel Chapman, Ichabod Hinckley.

1736 Samuel Chapman, John Huntington, Zebulon West.
1737 "   Joseph Hatch,   "
1738 "   Zebulon West, Timothy Hatch.
1739 Joseph Baker, Ebenezer Nye, Samuel Chapman.
1740 Zebulon West,   "   "
1741 Samuel Chapman,   "   Zebulon West.
1742 "   "   "
1743 Ebenezer Nye, John Lathrop,   "
1744 "   "   "
1745 Zebulon West, Ebenezer Nye, John Lathrop.
1746 John Tyler, John Lathrop, Zebulon West.
1747 Zebulon West, John Tyler, Joshua Wills.
1748 "   "   "
1749 "   "   "
1750 "   "   "
1751 "   Joshua Wills, John Lathrop.
1752 "   "   John Stearns.
1753 Ebenezer Nye,   "   Zebulon West.
1754 Zebulon West, Ebenezer Nye, Joshua Wills.
1755 Ebenezer Nye, Joshua Wills, Joseph West.
1756 "   "   "
1757 Joseph West,   "   Samuel Chapman.
1758 Joshua Wills, Joseph West, Solomon Loomis.
1759 "   "   "
1760 Joseph West, Solomon Loomis, Ichabod Griggs.
1761 "   "   "
1762 "   "   "
1763 No record to be found.
1764 Ichabod Griggs, Elijah Chapman, Joseph Lathrop.
1765 "   "   "
1766 "   "   "
1767 "   "   "
1768 "   "   "
1769 Elijah Chapman, Joseph Lathrop, Stephen Steel.
1770 "   "   "
1771 "   "   "
1772 Joseph Lathrop, Stephen Steel, Samuel Chapman.
1773 Stephen Steel, Samuel Chapman, Solomon Wills.
1774 Solomon Wills, Caleb West, Samuel West.
1775 Samuel West, Jr., Samuel Chapman, Ichabod Hinckley.
1776 "   "   David Lathrop, Ichabod Hinckley, James West.
1777 Samuel West, Jr., James Chamberlin, Solomon Wills.
1778 "   Jonathan Wills, Samuel Cobb, Jr.
1779 Joshua Wills, Samuel Cobb, Jr., Joseph West, Daniel Edgerton.
1780 Joseph West, Daniel Edgerton, Samuel Cobb, Jr., Benoni Shepherd.
1781 Joseph West, Daniel Edgerton, Samuel Cobb, Jr., Benoni Shepherd, Ichabod Hinckley.

THE EARLY HISTORY OF TOLLAND. 145

1782	Ichabod Hinckley, Samuel Ladd, Joshua Griggs.	
1783	" " "	
1784	" " "	
1785	" " "	
1786	" " Simon Chapman.	
1787	Joshua Griggs, Daniel Edgerton, Samuel Ladd.	
1788	Ichabod Hinckley, Elnathan Strong, Daniel Edgerton.	
1789	" Daniel Edgerton, Elnathan Strong.	
1790	Daniel Edgerton, Simon Chapman, John Steel.	
1791	" " Samuel Ladd.	
1792	" " Ichabod Hinckley.	
1793	" Ichabod Hinckley, Simon Chapman.	
1794	" " "	
1795	" Samuel Ladd, Jonathan Barnes.	
1796	" " "	
1797	" " "	
1798	Jonathan Barnes, Daniel Edgerton, Ichabod Hinckley.	
1799	" John Kingsbury, Jabez West.	
1800	" Jeduthan Cobb, Jabez Kingsbury.	
1801	" " "	
1802	" Jabez Kingsbury, Jeduthan Cobb.	
1803	Jeduthan Cobb, Jonathan Barnes, Jabez Kingsbury.	
1804	Jonathan Barnes, Jeduthan Cobb, "	
1805	" " "	
1806	Jabez Kingsbury, " Simon Chapman, Jr.	
1807	Simon Chapman, Jr., " Ashbel Chapman.	
1808	Ashbel Chapman, " Ichabod Hinckley.	
1809	Eliakim Chapman, Ephraim West, Jabez Kingsbury.	
1810	Ashbel Chapman, Samuel Ladd, Ichabod Hinckley, John Warren, Ezra Chapman.	
1811	Calvin Willey, John Warren, Ezra Chapman, Aaron Chapman, Thomas Howard.	
1812	John Warren, Ezra Chapman, Aaron Chapman, Shubael Reed, John Stanley.	
1813	Ephraim West, Eliakim Chapman, Shubael Reed.	
1814	" Simon Chapman, Jr., Ashbel Steel.	
1815	" " "	
1816	Hezekiah Nye, Ezra Chapman, Ichabod Hinckley.	
1817	" Sylvanus Haynes, Joseph Howard.	
1818	" Eliphalet Young, Ezra Chapman.	
1819	Eliphalet Young, Ezra Chapman, Aaron Chapman.	
1820	Stephen Griggs, Ephraim West, John Kingsbury.	
1821	Ezra Chapman, William Tillinghast, George M. Hyde.	
1822	George M. Hyde, Hezekiah Nye, Cordial Newcomb.	
1823	" " "	
1824	" Cordial Newcomb, William A. Sumner.	
1825	" Seymour Fuller, Solomon Howe.	
1826	" " "	
1827	" Luther Eaton, Cordial Newcomb.	
1828	Cordial Newcomb, Eli Baker, Solomon Howe.	

19

1829 George M. Hyde, Eli Baker, Solomon Howe.
1830 Eli Baker, Hezekiah Nye, Samuel Kent.
1831 Samuel Kent, Cordial Newcomb, Loren P. Waldo.
1832 John Lyon, Loren P. Waldo, Ira K. Marvin.
1833 Loren P. Waldo, John Lyon, "
1834 " Novatus Chapman, Charles Fish.
1835 " " "
1836 Oliver Lord, Carlos Chapman, Ebenezer West.
1837 Solomon L. Griggs, Warren Fitch, Joseph Burnham.
1838 Loren P. Waldo, Solomon L. Griggs, "
1839 " " John W. Gager.
1840 " " "
1841 " Novatus Chapman, Luther C. Anderson.
1842 Luther C. Anderson, John W. Gager, Levi Drake.
1843 " Sherman Chapman, Wm. C. Newcomb.
1844 Loren P. Waldo, Nathaniel K. Sibley, Lucius S. Fuller.
1845 " " "
1846 Joseph Clark, Sheldon Eaton, Orrin Ward.
1847 Moses Underwood, John W. Gager, Samuel D. Merrick.
1848 William C. Newcomb, William Holman, Alvan Kibbe, 2d.
1849 " " "
1850 John P. Brigham, Obadiah P. Waldo, Seth Brown.
1851 " " "
1852 Benjamin L. Young, Orson A. Richardson, Wm. Clark, 2d.
1853 " " "
1854 Alvan P. Hyde, Charles Lathrop, Jabez West.
1855 Charles Underwood, Anthony M. Weaver, George Eaton.
1856 Lucius S. Fuller, Edward P. Kellogg, Edmund Joslin.
1857 " " "
1858 Sherman Chapman, Elijah S. Chapman, Porter Walbridge.
1859 " " "
1860 Charles Underwood, James M. Babcock, James I. Andrews.

GENERAL INDEX

ABBOT, Elizabeth 115 John
  Sr 115
ABBOTT, Abiel 129 Alexander
  129 Elizabeth 128 129
  Erastus 129 Jehiel 129
  John 7 8 50 128 129 John
  Jr 45 129 Lucius 129 Mrs
  Alexander 92 Nehemiah 129
  Polly 129 Sally 129 Sarah
  129 Temperance 129
ABBY, John 47
ABORN, Dan 131 Dorcas 131
  Dorothy 131 Elizabeth 131
  Hannah 131 Hiram 131
  Jedediah 131 John 131 John
  G 131 Laura 131 Lucius 131
  Madison 131 Maria 131
  Martha 131 Mary 131 Morton
  131 Parkel 131 Parkil 131
  Reuben 131 Roxy 131 Ruth
  131 Sally 131 Samuel 45
  130 131 Sarah 131
ADAMS John 47
AGARD, Mrs Mason 68
ALLEN, Amasa 50 Asa 56
  Eliab 56 Joshua 45 Maria
  131 Nathan 47 Squire 47
ALLYN, John 13 Matthew 8 11
  12 14
ALVORD, Anna 104 Saul Sr
  104
AMADON, Moses 50
ANDERSON, Luth C 142 Luther
  C 141 146
ANDREWS, James I 146
ARCHER, John 56
ARNOLD, Oliver 26
ASHLEY, Elijah 141
ATCHISON, John 45
BABCOCK, James M 146
BAKER, 12 Abigail 79 96
  Alice 80 Almira 80 Alvin
  79 Amelia 80 Ann 79 C L 43
  Celinde 80 Chauncey 80
  Daniel 45 78 Deborah 79
  Delight 79 Elizabeth 79

BAKER (continued)
  Ebenezer 78 Eli 79 141 145
  146 Florilla 80 Heman 79
  Heman Jr 50 58 79 Jacob 78
  Jeffrey 77 Jerusha 78
  Joanna 93 John 78-80
  Joseph 9 14 18 44 60 77-80
  143 144 Joseph Jr 78 79
  Juliana 80 Lois 79 Lydia
  79 80 Margaret 78 Mary 78
  Nancy 80 Oliver 79 Ruth 78
  Samuel 44 57 Sarah 78 Seth
  78 Seymour 80 Temperance
  129 Titus 52 60 78
BALDWIN, Asa 50 Col 68
BAPTIST CHURCH, 43
BARBER, Ansel S 68 104
  Benjamin 9 Mary 68
BARNARD, Aaron 88 Abby 89
  Ann 88 89 Esther 89
  Francis 89 Joel 56 John
  45-47 58 88 89 Jonathan 89
  Moses 58 88 89 Reuben 89
  Samuel 45 88 Sarah 31
  Solomon 89 Thomas 58 88 89
  Thos 58 William 55 56 89
BARNES, Elizabeth 113
  Jonathan 140 142 145
BARRETT, Bartholomew 13
BARROWS, Sylvester 43
BARTLETT, Samuel 45
BELBON, James 47
BELL, how procured 24
BENTON, Abigail 81 83 130
  Adonijah 82 Agnes 81
  Alfred 82 Alvin 82 83 Anna
  81 82 Austin 82 Azariah 50
  58 80-82 Azariah L 82
  Benjamin D 82 83 141 Betty
  81 Charles O 35 Charles
  West 83 Chester 81 Daniel
  18 58 80-82 102 143 Daniel
  Jr 91 Dorothy 82 Eleanor
  83 Elihu 82 Elijah 51 52
  81 Elisha 81 Elizabeth 83
  Erastus 82 Eunice 81

BENTON (continued)
George B 83 Huldah 83 Ira
82 Jacob 53 81 82 Jane 82
83 Jerusha 83 92 John 81
Jonathan 50 82 Joseph 8 18
19 21 28-30 83 109 110 143
Joseph Jr 12 80 Joseph Sr
12 80 Josiah 50 Juliana 83
Keziah 132 Levi 82 Mary 81
91 Mehitabel 83 Milton W
83 Minerva 83 Nathan 81
Ozias 82 83 Ozias Sr 82
Phebe 81 Prudence 83 Ruth
81 83 Samuel 15 18 45 50
80 82 143 Samuel Jr 12 45
80 82 87 Samuel Sr 12 80
82 Sarah 81-83 Silas 81
Solomon 82 Susalla 81
Thankful 82 Timothy 16 83
102 130 William 45 57 80
81 William A 82 Zadoc 56
82 Zadock 53
BETTY (Mulatto), 121
BEWTON, Elias 51
BICKNELL, Hannah 97
BIGELOW, Hannah 124
BILL, Jonathan 45 Joshua 45
BILLINGS, Samuel 56
BIRGE, Cornelius 5 9 12 18
Jonathan 45 Joseph 12
Lathrop 127
BISBEE, Joseph 47
BISHOP, Anna 31 Joseph 108
110 141 142 Mrs Joseph 64
72
BISSELL, Ephraim 12 Josiah
9
BLACKMAN, Samuel 47
BLACKMORE, Samuel 45
BLISS, Emeline Eliza 129
Jonathan 47 John 7 129 142
Jonathan 45 Judah 125 142
Mary Eliza 129 Sally 7 129
Samuel 47 Sarah Olivia 129
Sylvester 129
BOARDMAN, Nathn 45
BOLLES, Augustus 43
BOROUGHS, Jonathan 45
BOUNTIES TO SOLDIERS, 51-55

BOWEN, Henry 45
BRACE, Daniel 47 Nathaniel
45 Stephen 12 47 William W
110
BRADLEY, Elijah 50 George
18 Henry 47 Jabez 45 52
Jane 82 Josiah 50
BRAINARD, Nabby 108 Sally
108
BREED, 112
BREWER, Daniel 47 Thomas 47
BREWSTER, Daniel 45
BRIGHAM, John P 141 146
Mary 66
BRONSON, Beriah 45 Noadiah
47
BROOKS, Joel 47
BROWN, Alexander 50 Anna
133 Ebenezer 51 Jacob 50
Jacob 2d 50 James A 8 128
142 John 47 Jonah 50 Jude
50 Seth 146
BUCK, Amasa 50 Thomas 45
Thomas Jr 56
BUCKLAND, Jonathan 45
BUEL, Matthew 50 Miss 65
BUELL, Asenath 130 Joseph
45
BULL, Thomas 13
BURDON, Benjamin 45 Rinaldo
47
BURGESS, Lot 53 56
BURNET, Mary 84
BURNHAM, Gideon 47 Joseph
146 Thomas 9 12-14
BURNS, Thomas 45
BURRES, Jonathan 94
BURROUGH, Jonathan 50
BURROUGHS, John P 51
Jonathan 58 94 Sarah 81
BURROWS, Daniel 106 John 46
47 58 John P 51
BURT, David 36 Mary 36
Sarah 37
BURYING-GROUNDS, 101
CADWELL, Edmund 47
CADY, Abner 56 Elizabeth
123 Jedediah 56 John 70
CARLTON, David 50 John 50

CARLTON (continued)
 Lydia 65 Richard 50-52
CARPENTER, Allen 55
 Catherine 122 Com 50
 Comfort 50 Lois 79 Molly
 135 Nathan 50
CARVER, Samuel 45
CASE, Abigail 92 Ichabod 55
 Willliam 47
CASWELL, Matthew 12
CENSUS, 135
CENTER OF TOWN, 5
CHALKER, Alex 2s 47
CHAMBERLAIN, James 139
CHAMBERLIN, James 48 51 57
 77 144 Jas 52
CHAPIN, Abina 117 Bliss 81
 Eunice 81 Oliver 45
 Theodore 61 81
CHAPLIN, Noah 50
CHAPMAN, Aaron 64 65 67 145
 Abigail 68 Alexander 65
 Ariel 65 Ashbel 34 35 54
 64 66 140-142 145 Carlos
 65 68 141 142 Col 63
 Daniel 35 61 64 65 Dorcas
 64 E 51 71 E Sr 52 Edward
 62 Eliakim 63 67 140 145
 Elijah 31 48-50 54 57 59
 61 64 65 67 75 77 97 133
 139 144 Elijah Jr 140
 Elijah S 35 98 146 Elijh S
 142 Erastus 65 Esther 64
 133 Eunice 65 Ezra 68 140-
 142 145 Gen 24 Hannah 31
 65 66 Henry 9 65 Jacob 65
 James 143 Joanna 64 75 77
 John B 65 Lydia 65 Lydia M
 68 Margaret 66 125 Mary 64
 66 68 97 99 134 Nancy 64
 71 Nathan 65 Novatus 65 68
 141 142 146 Reuben 35 64
 97-99 Robert 68 Roxalana
 63 71 Roxana 64 Ruth 32 63
 64 66 Samuel 15 31 32 44
 45 49 56 57 61-67 81 122
 134 138-140 142-144 Samuel
 Jr 56 Samuel Sr 44 56 57
 125 Sarah 31 63 64 65 97

CHAPMAN (continued)
 Sherman 68 141 146 Shermn
 142 Simon 9 12 24 45 48 55
 61 65 145 Simon Jr 67 145
 Simon Sr 67 Solomon 64
 William 65
CHARTER, John 50
CHASE, Samuel 53 56
CHURCH, when organized, 29
CLARK, Joseph 141 146 Mary
 90 William 2d 141 Wm 2d
 146
CLASSES TO OBTAIN SOLDIERS,
 55
CLEAVELAND, Hannah 95
COBB, Achsah 98 Alma 98
 Almy 125 Amos 58 59 97 Ann
 97 Betsey 98 Calvin P 98
 Daniel 97 98 David 97
 Eliza 98 Elizabeth 98
 Elvira 97 98 Esther 97
 Hannah 97 98 Hope 97
 Horace 98 Jeduthan 97 140
 145 Luther 98 Mary 64 97-
 99 Mary Ann 98 Moses 97
 Pamela 97 Rachel 97 98
 Ruth 97 98 117 Samuel 34
 47-49 52 58 64 97 99 117
 125 138 139 142 Samuel Jr
 97 144 Sarah 34 97 Solomon
 97 Waite 98 William 97 98
 125 Wm Bicknell 98
COGSWELL, Eunice Anna 133 H
 128 Joseph 51
COLTON, Samuel 47
COLTRAIN, William 56
CONANT, Joseph 45
CONTROVERSY CONCERNING
 TITLE, 14
CONVERSE, Dorothy 33
COOK, Daniel 9 12 18 30
 Ebenezer 9 50 Lydia 84
 Nathaniel 9 Samuel 134
COOLEY, George 45 Mary H 41
 Noah 50
CORY, Damaris 36
COTTON, Samuel 47
COVENTRY TOWN LINE, 17
COVIL, James 55

COWEN, Mary 77
COY, Moses 55 Samuel 12
CRAFTS, Hannah 95
CRANDAL, Abel 51 Amos 86
 Bethiah 86 Const 47
 Constant 86 Giles 86
 Jarvis 33 86 Joel 53
 Minerva 33 Richmond 50
 Roxana 86 Samuel 86
CRANDALL, Abel 51 Alden B
 15 Constant 46 58 Jemima
 135 John 52
CRAW, Sally 132
CREASY, Jonathan 56
CROCKER, Joseph 45
CROSS, John 47 Talmon 141
 142
CROSWELL, John 47 Joseph 47
CROWELL, Manoah 53
CROWN POINT, expedition to,
 44
CUBA, 46
CURTIS, John 47 Lydia 104
CUSHMAN, Eliphalet 50
DANA, Ebenezer 47 Isaac 47
DANIELS, Joel 45 47
DARLING, Samuel 45
DART, Chester 131 Jonathan
 45 Laura 131
DAVIS, Isaac 78 Job 56
 Joseph 45 Martin 51 Samuel
 56 Sarah 78
DAY, Charles 50 Sarah 82
 Stephen 48 51 52
DEED TO FIRST PROPRIETORS,
 10
DELANO, Aaron 53 115 Amos
 115 Amy 93 114 121 Ann 114
 Anne 114 115 Barnabas 114
 115 Clarinda 114 Elizabeth
 84 114 115 Esther 114
 Gideon 115 Jabez 114
 Jethro 114 Joan 114 Joanna
 116 John 114 Jonathan 52
 84 101 102 109 114-116
 121-123 143 Joseph 115
 Luther 53 56 58 Mary 118
 Moses 56 115 Nathan 114
 Nathaniel 115 Philip 114

DELANO (continued)
 Prudence 114 Ruth 114
 Sarah 114-116 Susanna 114
 122 123 Sylvanus 84 114
 115 Thomas 114 Timothy 45
 114 Zebulon 114
De la NOYE, Philip 115
DeLAYNAYE, Philip 115
DeWOLF, Charles 55
DIGGINS, Abigail 113
DIMICK, Elizabeth 79 John
 56 Shubael 45 51 52
DIMOCK, Sally 66 Samuel 55
DIMROCK, Edward 50
DOLLABY, John 47
DOMESTIC MANUFACTURES, 60
DONATION, to Boston 48 to
 New London 49
DOWLING, Thomas 43
DOWNING, Cornelius 47
 Reuben 47
DOYLE, John 64
DRAKE, Joseph 12 18 Levi
 146 Nathaniel 9
DRESSER, Joseph A 110 Mrs
 Joseph A 134
DUNHAM, Sarah 76
DURPHY, Elijah 47
EARL, Moses 47
EATON, Aaron 46 47 58 86
 Almandor 85 Ann 84 Anna 85
 Bethiah 84 86 Clarissa 85
 Daniel 12 14 19 84 94 100
 143 Doct 135 Ebenezer 84
 100 Elizabeth 84 86 115
 Epaphras 84 George 142 146
 Horatio D 85 Jasper 85
 Jeduthan C 88 106 Jemima
 71 84 86 122 John 45
 Joseph 45 Juda 84 Luther
 85 105 108 109 115 145
 Lydia 84 Mary 84 86 Moses
 86 Mr 28 Oliver 62 85
 Peter 84 Rachel 84 Ralph
 85 Sally 85 Samuel 84 86
 Samuel Sr 86 Sheldon 146
 Solomon 50 51 55 59 84-86
 115 Thomas 86 William 12
 18 21 29 46 47 58 84-87

EATON (continued)
100 143 William W 141 142
Wm 58 Zerad 85
EDGAR, Thomas 9
EDGERTON, Amaret Grant 100
Anna 100 Austin 100 Betsey
100 Daniel 25 52 97 99 100
140 142 144 145 Daniel Jr
99 Edna 100 Eliza Ann 100
Erastus 99 100 Freelove
100 Hezekiah 100 Joseph 47
Levi 98-100 Linus 100
Lucius 100 Marvin 100 Mary
97 99 Mrs Dwight 98 Mrs
Levi 123 Phebe 99 100 123
Reuben 98-100 Sally 66
Sarah 99 Sarah Kingsbury
100 William L 100 Wm L 142
EDSON, Eliab 56
EGGLESTON, Thomas 9
ELDREDGE, Elizabeth 40
William 56 141
ELLIS, Thomas 12 18 William
47
ELLSWORTH, John 11 12 72
Jonathan 12 Samuel 9
ELMER, Deborah 135 William
50
EMMONS, Peter 12 143
ENO, John 9
EVANS, Timothy 47
FARNSWORTH, Thomas 9
FELLOWS, 62 Abigail 75 Amos
57 58 75 Isaac 50 59 75
Jacob 45 Ruth 75 Stephen
75
FELT, Samuel 50
FENTON, Adonijah 50 Asa 50
FIELDS, Josiah 45
FISH, Charles 146
FISHING IN WILLIMANTIC
RIVER, 16
FITCH, Joseph 13 Warren 142
146
FLINT, Hannah 88
FLYNT, Jonathan R 142
Nathan 102
FOOT, Ephraim 47
FORBES, Abraham 47

FORD, John 45
FORT WILLIAM HENRY, 45
FORWARD, Samuel 5 12
FRANTZ, Christopher 50
FULLER, Benjamin 141 142
David 47 Huldah 125 John
45 Lucius S 141 146 Mrs
Lucius S 8 129 Seymour 145
Solomon L 142
FURMAN, Israel 56 John 50
GAGE, Sylvanus 53 55
GAGER, John W 142 146
GAYLORD, Jonas 9
GEORGE (king of England),
20
GIBBS, Abigail 78 Bathsheba
118 Margaret 78
GILBERT, Lois 79 Wyllys 142
GILLETT, Cornelius 9 Nathan
5 12 Nathaniel Jr 9
GLEASON, Jedutn 142
GOFF, Stephen 47
GOODRICH, Josiah 142 143
GORDON, John 45
GOWDY, Alexander 45
GRANT, Adoniram 52 122 Ann
123 Ebenezer 50 100 123
Edna 100 123 Edwin L 35
134 Edwin Lathrop 123
Elias 123 Elisha 123 Eliza
123 Elizabeth 123 Ephraim
97 100 109 122 123 Ephraim
Jr 123 Esther 97 123
Eunice 123 George M 35 123
134 Grace 123 Harry 123
Juliana 123 Martha 122
Mary 123 Nathaniel 9 12 18
115 Noah 5 7 9 12 18 19 21
30 122 123 143 Oliver 123
Phebe 123 Philip 123
Prudence 123 Samuel 9
Solomon 122 123 Stephen
123 Susanna 122 Thomas 5 7
Thomas Jr 7 William 123
Zebulon 123
GRAY, John 45 Lucy 95
GREEN, Jonas 61 Timothy 56
GRIDLEY, John 9
GRIGGS, Anna 76 Austin 76

GRIGGS (continued)
  Betsey 76 77 Boswell 75 76
  Charles 75 76 Charles G 76
  Chauncey 76 77 141 142
  Chester 76 Daniel 75 76
  Elijah 75 Elijah Chapman
  76 Eliza 76 Eunice Hovey
  76 Harriet 76 Henry O 76
  Ichabod 47 57 58 75 76 99
  139 144 Ichabod 1st 77
  Ichabod 2d 77 Ichabod Jr
  75 James Randolph 76
  Joanna 75 77 Joseph 76
  Joshua 50 57 75-77 141 145
  Julia 76 Lemuel P 76
  Leverett 76 114 Lucius 76
  Mary 76 Matta 76 Mercy 76
  77 Minerva 76 Mrs Leverett
  114 Nancy 76 Normand
  Brigham 76 Parmela Porter
  76 Ralph 76 Ralph R 77 142
  Roswell Leonard 76 Roxey
  Chpaman 33 Sally 76 Samuel
  76 Sarah 75 76 99 Seth D
  77 141 142 Seth Dunham 76
  Solo L 33 Solomon L 146
  Solomon Lathrop 76 77
  Stephen 76 77 92 145
  Susannah 75
GRISWOLD, Daniel Jr 9
  Simeon 50 Thomas 9
GROSVENOR, Jacob 37 Mary 36
  37 Mary-Williams 37 Ruth
  37 William 37 Wm 36
GROVER, Abigail 134 Aner
  141 Daniel 142 Daniel 2d
  141 Leonard 46 47 58 94
  Michael 47
GUERNSEY, Ezekiel 47
HALL, Eliakim 38 John 18 19
  Mary 36 Mr 20 Samuel 45
HAMLIN, Levi 50
HAMMOND, Eleazar Jr 52
  Titus 53
HANKS, Mr 26
HARRIS, Amos 52 Brisley 51
  Bristo 121 Silas 47
HART, Medad 54
HARVEY, Eunice 132 Nathan

HARVEY (continued)
  45
HASKELL, Elijah 51 Jacob 51
  52 John 55
HASTINGS, Geo D 142
HATCH, Abigail 89-92
  Abithea 90 Abner 50 90 91
  Amy 16 90 118 Anna 66 90
  92 Asenath 91 Bathsheba 91
  Bethiah 90 Betsey 90
  Caroline 91 Clarissa 91
  Dan 50 90 Dana 90 Daniel
  89 Darius 92 David 45 91
  92 Deborah 92 Ebenezer 90
  Edward 46 47 Edy 51 55 56
  91 Eleazar 53 56 91
  Eleazar Lathrop 91 Ephraim
  90 Esther 91 Eunice 135
  Experience 91 Frank 90 92
  George 92 Grace 91 Gustin
  91 Hannah 91 Heman 92
  Honora 92 Ichabod 58 89 92
  100 Isaac 90 Jedida 92
  Jeduthan 91 Jerusha 91
  Jethro 92 Job 92 Jonathan
  90 91 133 Joseph 12 15 18
  19 43 44 66 77 89-92 118
  143 144 Joseph 2d 76 90
  116 Joseph 3d 90 Joseph Jr
  58 Judah 46 47 58 89
  Justus 89 92 Lectana 91
  Lemuel 45 90 Lovisa 91
  Lucy 91 92 Marvin 91 Mary
  76 90-92 116 Mary Hyde 91
  Mercy 77 90 96 Morana 91
  Nathaniel 91 Nersa 91
  Prudence 91 Rebecca 90
  Rosamond 91 Ruth 89 90 92
  Sally 90 Saluenius 92
  Sarah 90 91 Semantha 91
  Solomon 92 Thankful 91
  Timothy 90 92 144 William
  58 90 Zadoc 91 Zerviah 89
HATCHE, Ede 56
HAWKINS, Mrs A M 85
HAYNES, Joseph 13 Sylvanus
  145
HAYWARD, Henry 13 Joseph 47
HEATH, Isaac 58 Joseph 45

HEATH (continued)
  Reuben 58
HERINGTON, Timothy 56
HERO, John 47
HETON, S 112
HICKS, Charles R 103 Mrs
  Charles R 113
HIGHWAY, first location of,
  4
HILL, Henry 49
HILLIARD, Miner 54
HILLS, Isaac 45 Jacob 45
HINCKLEY, Anna 74 Benjamin
  74 Bethiah 74 Daniel 74
  David 50 Deborah 74 Hannah
  74 Ichabod 45 51 53 55 57
  74 76 138 139 143-145
  Ichabod Jr 74 Mary 74 76
  97 Sarah 74 Temperance 74
HINSDALE, Barnabas 12 102
HOBART, Prudence 114
HOCKINS, William 45
HOLBROOK, Caroline 91 Elias
  52 Elizabeth 98
HOLCOMB, Benaiah 9
HOLLISTER, Asabel 47 Asahel
  47 Jacob 47 Robert 47
HOLMAN, Mrs William 130
  Thomas 43 William 141 146
HOLMES, Ebenezer 47 Ezra 50
  Walter 55 56
HOLT, Nathaniel 47 Philemon
  56
HORTON, Capt 68
HOSKINS, Anthony 9
HOWARD, Aurelia 36 Joseph
  106 109 145 Thomas 145
HOWE, Solomon 145 146
HUBBARD, George 51 52
  Hannah 96 Isaac 102
HULL, 42
HUNT, John 43 Medad 55
HUNTINGTON, Abigail 33 72
  73 Almira 73 Ambrose 73
  Andrew 72 73 Appollos 73
  Christopher 12 72 Deborah
  72 73 Diantha 73 Elias 73
  Elisha 73 Ephraim Newell
  73 Esther 73 Frederick

HUNTINGTON (continued)
  Augustus 73 Hezekiah 53 56
  73 74 Jane 73 Jerusha 73
  John 9 12 15 33 43 44 50
  61 72-74 109 114 115 142-
  144 Laura 73 Lucia 73 Mara
  73 Maria 73 Martha 122
  Mehitabel 73 74 Nancy 73
  Rebecca 73 Robert Goodloe
  73 Ruth 73 Samuel 45 56 57
  72 73 Samuel H 74 Thankful
  72 73 William 51 73
HUTCHINS, Joshua 45
HUTCHINSON, Samuel 45
HYDE, Alvan P 142 146 Alvin
  P 141 George M 141 142 145
  146 Samuel 47
INCORPORATION, act of, 10
INDIAN, names 17 tribes 12
INGHAM, Mary 131
INMAN, Israel 56
ISHAM, Abby Jane 128
  Abigail 128 Asher 127
  Chester C 128 David B 128
  Gordon 110 Gurdon 110 127
  128 142 Harriet A 128
  James 127 John 45 Mary 128
  Minerva 76 Mrs Oliver K 77
  O K 76 Oliver K 109 110
  141 Oliver Kingsley 128
  Polly 127 128 Shubael 128
  Shubael S 128
JAMES, Amos 52
JENNINGS, Eunice 39 Nathan
  50 Thomas 70
JEWETT, Alice 80 David 52
JOHNSON, Abner 55 56 Anna
  85 115 Caleb 50 Daniel 50
  David 85 Elihu 45 51 59
  Mary 134 Noah 55 Samuel 50
  Sarah 110 William 51 53 56
JOHNSTON, Jonathan 47
JONES, Lemuel 45
JOSLIN, Edmund 146
JOSLYN, Mrs Edmund 98
KEELER, Sarah 64
KEITH, William 108
KELLOGG, Daniel 109 142
  Edward P 146

KEN, Samuel 109
KENT, Elizabeth S 35 72
  Elizabeth Sophronia 33 127
  James S 33 105 James Steel
  127 Melicent Wills 33 126
  Mr 127 S 33 Samuel 33 126
  146
KIBBE, Alvan 2d 146 Alvin
  131 Alvin 2d 141 Hannah
  131 Mrs Alvin 131
KIBBEE, Bidad 50 Daniel 50
  James 45 50
KILBOURN, Eliphalet 55 56
KIMBALL, Benjamin 53
  William 47
KIMBERLY, Mr 19 Thomas 18
KING, Charles 45 Hezekiah
  45
KINGSBURY, Anna 66 Eleazar
  52 54 Geo H 142 George
  Henry 66 Hannah 65 74
  Jabez 25 65 66 92 140 142
  145 John 66 145 John
  Brigham 66 Mary 66 Mrs
  George H 35 Nathaniel 65
  74 Nathaniel Jr 25 Ruth 65
  83 S R 83 Sally 66 Samuel
  65 Sarah 65 66 Susannah
  124
KINGSLEY, Polly 128
KNAPPING, Thomas 47
LADD, Abigail 124 Ahijah
  124-126 Ahijah Jr 125 Almy
  125 Alvan 125 Ann 114 Anna
  102 124 Ariel 102 124 141
  142 Charles Ahijah 125
  Daniel 124 125 David 124
  Doct 126 Eliab 102 124 125
  Elisha 124 Elizabeth 124
  Ephraim 124 Esther 73 123
  125 Eunice 124 125 Ezekiel
  124 125 Ezra 125 Hannah
  124 Huldah 125 Jacob 66
  125 Jesse 124 Joel 125
  John 124 125 Jonathan 52
  102 124 Jonathan Jr 45 81
  102 124 125 Jonathan Sr
  124 125 Joseph 124 Lathrop
  125 Laura 125 Levi 125

LADD (continued)
  Lois 125 Lucy 124 Lura 124
  Luther 124 125 Lydia 124
  Margaret 66 125 Maria 125
  Mary 66 124 125 Mrs Doctor
  98 Presinda 124 Rachel 96
  Roxy 124 Ruth 66 124 125
  Samuel 52 54 66 109 123-
  125 140 145 Sarah 81 124
  Stephen 124 142 Susalla
  124 Susanna 124 Susannah
  124 Theodore Stearns 125
  Timothy 45 Wareham 66 125
  William C 141 William Cobb
  125 Zuriah 124
LAFAYETTE, 57 61 85 Gen 105
LAMB, Joseph 56
LANGWORTHY, Benj 47
LANMAN, James 107
LASSELL, James 88
LATHROP, Abigail 75 96 116
  Amelia 96 Anna 95 96 100
  Azel 96 Benjamin 95 Betsey
  76 77 Charles 97 141 146
  Daniel 99 David 94 144
  Deborah 96 Edna 96 123
  Elizabeth 34 71 95 121
  Elvira 95 Grace 96 Grant
  96 Hannah 94-96 Hope 15 25
  26 33 45 48 52 54 76 77 94
  96 123 139 143 Hope Sr 96
  Horace 95 96 Ichabod 75 96
  116 John 45 58 59 71 75
  94-97 99 138 142 144 John
  Jr 95 124 Jonathan 95
  Joseph 91 96 144 Julius 96
  Justin 97 Kelsey 96 Laura
  96 Lt 57 Lucy 59 95 Lydia
  95 Mary 95 96 Mary
  Angeline 97 Melatiah 96
  Mercy 96 Molly 95 Mr 60
  Nathaniel 96 Presenda 95
  Prudence 96 122 Rachel 96
  Rebecca 33 96 Rollin 95
  Rowland 95 141 Samuel M 97
  Sarah 96 99 Solomon 76 96
  Sophia 96 Susalla 95 124
  Thacher 45 Thankful 96
  Thatcher 95 Thomas

LATHROP (continued)
  Cleaveland 95 Wealthy R 97
  William 95 96 Zebulon 97
  99 100
LAWRENCE, Edward 50
LEE, 42
LEWIS, John 50
LITTLE, Martha 39
LOCATION OF TOWN, 18
LOOMER, H 9
LOOMIS, Abigail 90 134
  Alanson 135 Almon 134 Ann
  88 Anna 134 Ashbel 135
  Caroline 135 Daniel 9
  David 9 Deborah 135
  Ebenezer 135 Eleazar 135
  Eleazer 135 Elisha 134 135
  Elizabeth 135 Elmer 134
  Enoch 5 12 18 134 Epaphras
  66 134 Esther 134 135
  Eunice 135 Frances Eliza
  135 Grace 135 Hannah 135
  Hepzibah 135 Hezekiah 134
  135 Ichabod 9 Jeduthan 134
  135 Jemima 135 Joshua 5 9
  12 18 134 135 Justin 134
  Luke 66 134 Luther 135
  Mary 66 134 135 Mary
  Chapman 135 Minerva 135
  Molly 135 Moses 12 134
  Nathaniel 134 Priscilla
  135 Ralph 134 Ruth 134
  Sally 135 Samuel 135 Simon
  66 134 135 Solomon 45 53
  66 88 89 91 134 144
  Stephen 9
LORD, Miss 64 Oliver 141
  142 146 Richard 13
LOUISBURG, expedition to,
  44
LOVELAND, Lot 47 Mr 131
LOVEMAN, Benjamin 47
LUCAS, Christopher 47
LUCE, Jane 87 Jonathan 51
  59 Joseph 45 Joshua 87
  Leverett 87
LYON, John 142 146 John S
  142
McNEIL, Henry 56

MARKHAM, Abijah 45
MARSH, Abram 41 Jasper 56
  Mary H 41 Rhoda 41
MARSHALL, Daniel 112 Samuel
  9
MARVIN, Edwin E 142 Ira K
  141 146
MASON, Myron L 142
MATHER, Joseph 18
MATTHEWSON, Percival 43
MEETING-HOUSE, 21
MERRICK, Elizabeth 130 Saml
  D 142 Samuel D 146
METHODIST CHURCH, 42
MILITARY, 43
MILLER, Eunice 113
MILLS, Jedidiah 9 Melicent
  104
MINER, Andrew 50 51 Boswell
  52 Clement 51-53 56
MINISTERS, 28
MIX, Stephen 70
MIXTER, George 43
MONTCALM, Gen 45
MOORE, John 10
MOREY, 60
MORGAN, Abigail 68 George
  87
MORSE, Joshua 42 112
MUNSELL, Lois 93
NASH, Ansel 29 36 39 Eunice
  39 John 39 Martha 39 Mr 40
  41
NEGUS, John 47
NEWCOMB, Cordial 141 145
  146 Sarah 129 William C
  146 Wm C 141 146
NEWELL, Jacob 45 Rebecca 73
NEWTON, Elias 50 51
NOBLE, Gideon 36
NORRIS, Benjamin 54 Hope 97
NORTHROP, Sarah 88
NYE, Abel 130 Abigail 130
  Anna 130 Anne 130 Asenath
  130 Austin 130 Bathsheba
  130 Benjamin 129 Buell 130
  Ebenezer 12 18 44 129 130
  138 143 144 Ebenezer Jr
  130 Elizabeth 129 130

NYE (continued)
 Elizur 130 Eunice 129
 George 45 52 Harriet 130
 Hezekiah 130 141 145 146
 Horace 130 Jeduthan 130
 John 129 John Hyde 130
 Joseph 130 Lois 129
 Malatiah 129 Marvin 130
 Samuel 52 129 130 Sarah
 117 129 130 Susanna 130
 Sylvia 129 Thankful 118
 129
OFFICERS IN THE WARS, 57 58
OLCOTT, Titus 45
OLMSTED, Nicholas 13
ORCUTT, Ben Jones 56
 Benjamin Jones 56 Caleb 50
 Jacob 50 John 50
ORMS, Richard 47
PACK, Joseph 16 18 29 44 87
 88 Margaret 16 87
PALMER, John 52 Mr 112 Wait
 42 111
PARISH, Jere S 142 Jeremiah
 60 141 142
PARK, Joseph 143 Samuel 56
PARKER, Abel 50 Elizabeth
 86 Jona 50 Robert 97
 Samuel 19
PARKS, Joshua 50 Samuel 55
 Sarah 90
PARSONS, 62 Luke 45 Solomon
 56
PART, John 47
PATENT, 19
PAULK, 112 Abigail 132
 Amelia 96 Ammi 50 51 96
 132 133 Asenath 133
 Aurelia 133 David 132
 Dinah 132 Edwin 132
 Eliakim 132 Ephraim 132
 133 Erastus 133 Esther 133
 Eunice 132 134 Eunice Anna
 133 George 133 George M
 132 Grace 132 James 132
 Jeduthan 133 Jemima 132
 John 87 132 Jonathan 133
 Julius 132 Julius A 132
 Keziah 87 132 133 Laura

PAULK (continued)
 132 Lois 132 Lydia 132 133
 Margaret 132 Mary 132
 Micajah 133 Nathan L 133
 Noah 132 Puhamah 132 Ruth
 132 133 Sally 132 Samuel
 12 131 132 Sarah 132
 Zechariah 133
PAYNE, Brinton 45
PEARCE, Juliana 123
PEASE, Abner 45 50 Charles
 56 James 45
PECK, Elizabeth 115 Joseph
 12
PELTON, Moses 50
PERSONS WHO DIED IN ARMY,
 57 58
PETERS, John S 107 John
 Thompson 106
PETERSON, Andrew 51
PETITION, for new town 8 by
 town of East Windsor 9 de
 Coventry lands 18
PHELPS, Jonathan 45 Joseph
 9 William 9
PHILIPS, Jeremiah 56 Samuel
 56
PHILLIPS, Jeremiah 56
PIERCE, David 52
PIERSON, Nathan 74 142
PIKE, Joseph 45
PINNEY, Humphrey 9 Jonathan
 9 Nancy 76 Nathaniel 9
 Peter 50 Samuel 12 Samuel
 Jr 5
PITKIN, Ozias 70 William 13
PORTER, Abraham 47 Daniel 9
 12 Hezekaih 5 Hezekiah 5
 12 18 Joseph 5 9 18
 Nathaniel 9 Ruth 31
POST, Anna 82 Azariah 52
 Dorothy 131
POST-OFFICE, 103
PRATT, Daniel 45 Edy 56
PRESTON, Eunice 65 Tyrus 50
 51
PRICE, Rufus 50-52
PRISONERS IN TOLLAND, 60
PROUT, Joseph 47

PUTNAM, Israel 46 47 Maj 44
QUOTA OF TROOPS, 54
RAWDON, Ezra 53 56 Roxana 86
RAYMOND, Matthew 47
RAYNER, 42
READ, John 47
REDINGTON, Nathaniel 47 Olive 121
REED, Samuel 53 56 Shubael 145
RICE, Daniel 50 Joseph 18 Stephen 50
RICHARDS, Betty 81 James 13
RICHARDSON, Orson A 141 146 Sanford 56 Susanna 92
RIDER, Jeremiah 50
RILEY, Ackley 47
RIPPONER, John 47
ROBERTS, Daniel 47
ROBINSON, Elijah 139 Reuben 56
ROCKWELL, Joseph 7-9 18 Joseph Jr 5 7 12 Josiah 5 115 Samuel 9 12
ROLLS, Capt Samuel Chapman 45 Capt Samuel Stoughton 45 Capt Solomon Wills 50 Lieut Solomon Wills 47
ROOT, Joseph 50 Nathan 50 Thomas 19
ROSE, Thomas 47
ROYCE, Joseph 12
RUSSELL, Sarah 131 William 45
SABIN, Nehemiah 50 51
SAMPSON, Jonathan 47
SANFORD, Rebecca 110
SANGER, Jedediah 47
SAUNDERS, Israel 47
SCHUYLER, Col 44
SCOTT, Abigail 83 Mr 58 Oliver 55
SCRIPTER, John 50
SEARS, Homer 43
SEPARATISTS, 42
SETTLEMENT OF TOWN, 15
SEXTON, Elijah 50 Joseph 50
SHAW, Benjamin 47 Ebenezer

SHAW (continued) 47
SHEPARD, Anna 104 Anson 104 Benoni 52 54 103 104 109 Benoni A 104 Caleb 47 Desire 104 Eunice 104 Jonathan 103 Lydia 104 Pamela 104 Sally 104 Sophia 104
SHEPERD, Benoni 144
SHEPHERD, Benjamin 45
SHORT, Rhoda 41
SHORVEL, Charles 47
SHURTLIFF, Amos 47 John 50 Lathrop 45
SIBLEY, Nathaniel K 146
SIMONS, Hannah 32 Joshua 55 56
SKINNER, Joseph 9 Mary 81
SLAFTER, Anthony 18 Joseph 18 Sarah 132
SLAP, John 44
SLATE, Ann 97 John 97 Sarah 97
SLUMAN, Mary 118
SMITH, Col 105 Eli Ives 104 Elijah 60 104 140 Elijah Wills 104 Joel 79 Lydia 104 Lydia Melicent 104 Mary Mindwell 104 Melicent 104 Moses 104 Philip 9 Samuel 47
SNOW, Bilarky 120 Billaky 19
SOWLE, William 51
SPALDING, Nathan 73
SPARKS, Isiah 50 Jeremiah 50 Joseph 51 52
SPARROW, Asenath 130 Emeline 130 George 130 George E 130 James 130 John 130
SPENCER, Col 50 Hezekiah 45 Joseph 45
SQUIER, Abner 55 Isaac 51 James 43
STANLEY, Abigail 78 Jerusha 78 John 78 145 Nathaniel 70 Roswell 78 Samuel 47 78

STANLEY (continued)
Sanford 78 Sidney 78 142
STAPLES, Amos 47 Isaac 47
STARK, John 47
STEARNS, Abigail 113
  Charles 53 113 Daniel 113
  David 113 Ebenezer 110
  Eleanor 113 Elisha 113
  140-142 Elizabeth 110 113
  128 129 Elvira 97 98
  Eunice 113 Hannah 87 110
  114 Isaac 110 John 87 98
  113 114 129 144 John Jr 45
  Lydia 113 Martha 110 Mary
  110 113 Peter 110 Rebecca
  110 Rev Mr 112 Ruth 113
  Samuel 110 Sarah 110 113
  Shubael 12 14 18 87 109
  110 114 133 143 Shubael Jr
  42 110 111 113 Shubael Sr
  110 113
STEBBINS, Ebenezer 51 Ebenr
  51 Elisha 50
STEEL, Aaron 31-33 58
  Abigail 32-34 Andrew 33 34
  53 Ann 32 Anna 31 Ashbel
  32 33 126 145 Ashbel Smith
  33 Bethiah 31 Clarissa 32
  Daniel 32 David 32 Deborah
  33 Dorothy 33 Eleazar 33
  47-49 51 52 54 66 109 139
  Eleazer 31 33 34 Eleazer
  Jr 33 Elisha 31 34 139 142
  Elizabeth 32-34 Eunice 34
  Florilla 33 George 31 33
  Hannah 31 32 66 James 31
  33 34 58 Jas Jr 50
  Jeduthan 32 33 Joel 32 33
  John 31 33 34 45 52 55 145
  Juliana 32 Lovine 34
  Lusalla 32 Mara 34 Marilla
  33 Mary 32 34 Mary-ann 34
  Mehitabel 31 34 73 74
  Melicent Wills 33 126
  Minerva 33 Mr 28 Oliver W
  35 Oliver Wolcott 34
  Orrenda 32 Perez 32 50
  Rachel 34 Ralph 33 Rebecca
  33 Rev Mr 42 Roger Wolcott

STEEL (continued)
  34 Roxey Chapman 33 Ruth
  31-34 66 Salmon 33 Samuel
  32 33 50 53 58 Sanford 33
  35 Sarah 31 34 64 Seth
  Dwight 33 Stephen 20 28
  30-36 49 52 64 73 83 102
  111 114 133 144 Stephen Jr
  31 66 Zadoc 33 34
STEEPLE, when built, 24
STEVENS, Henry 50
STILES, Henry Jr 9 John 143
  Samuel 47 Thomas 9
STIMPSON, Hannah 87 James
  18 Noah 87
STIMSON, Aaron 88 Abel 55
  88 Alice 88 David 88 Eneas
  87 88 Gideon 88 Hannah 87
  88 114 Ichabod 87 132
  James 80 87 88 101 102 114
  Jane 87 Joel 50 88 John 88
  Joseph 88 Joshua 88 Keziah
  87 Lois 88 Margaret 87 88
  132 Miriam 88 Naomi 87
  Noah 46 47 58 87 88 Ruth
  88 Sarah 88 Simeon 50
  Simon 51 88 Stephen 52 54
  87 88 Thomas 87 88
STOCKING, Bethiah 31 Samuel
  31
STONE, Nathaniel 47
STORRS, Zalmon A 142
STOUGHTON, Israel 9 Samuel
  45 81 Thomas 12 18
STRAIT, Joseph A 141
STRICKLAND, Simon 47
STRONG, Abigail 118 121 128
  134 Elnathan 52 145 Joseph
  19 Lois 117 Nathan 37
  Nehemiah 36
SUMNER, William 142 William
  A 145
TALCOTT, David 45 Gov 70
  John 13
TAYLOR, Nathaniel 12 18 116
  143 Samuel 56 Stephen 50
THACHER, Hepzibah 135
THOMAS, Caleb 56
THOMPSON, Gurdon 140 Justus

THOMPSON (continued) 50
THRALL, Moses 45 Timothy 8 11
TIFFANY, Nathan 45
TILDEN, Joseph 45 92
TILLINGHAST, Joseph 43 William 145
TOWN-CLERKS, 109
TRUESDALE, Jos 47
TRYON, Mrs George 129
TUCKER, Ephraim 12 Joseph 45
TYLER, Anna 124 John 52 144
UNDERWOOD, Charles 146 Henry 108 Heny 142 Moses 146
UTLEY, Samuel 12
WADSWORTH, James 18 19 Mr 20
WAKEFIELD, Abigail 34
WALBRIDGE, Porter 142 146
WALDO, Bethuel 93 94 Bethuel Sr 93 94 Cornelius 93 Edward 93 94 Ezra 46 47 58 93 Henry 94 John 93 Lemuel 94 Lois 93 Loren P 141 142 146 Obadiah P 108 141 142 146
WALKER, Levi Jr 43
WALLIS, Nathaniel 7 12 124 130
WARD, Amos 45 Jacob 45 Orrin 141 142 146
WARREN, John 141 142 145 Nathaniel 45 Robert 9 Thankful 72
WASHBURN, Elijah 50 Luke 50 William 56
WASHINGTON, George 72
WATERS, Hezekiah 45 Thomas 45
WATKINS, Brodwell 56
WATSON, Nathaniel 9
WAY, Ebenezer 13 John 47
WEAVER, Anthony M 146
WEBB, Abner 45
WEBSTER, Milton 83 Minerva 83 Simeon 45

WELLS, Hezekiah 45 James 104
WEST, Abigail 116 118 121 122 Abina 117 Abner 45 116 Alden 117 Alice 122 Amasa 115 118 Amy 114 118 121 Ann 116 118 Anna 116 118 Bathsheba 91 116 118 Beulah 118 Bicknell 117 Caleb 118 122 144 Carlo 117 Catherine 122 Charles 117 121 Chauncey 117 Chloe 121 Christopher 114 115 121 Daniel 121 Deborah 116 Desire 104 118 Dorcas 117 118 Dorothy 122 Dura 122 Ebenezer 118 122 141 142 146 Eleazar 121 Eli S 117 Elijah 118 121 Elisha 116 117 Elizabeth 121 Ephraim 16 97 115-118 140 145 Esther 121 Eunice 117 121 Evaline 117 Frances 94 Francis 14 15 19 20 45 115 116 118 119 121 143 Frederick 116 Grace 116 117 Hannah 117 121 122 Henry W 117 142 Ichabod 53 55 Ira 122 Irena 118 Irene 122 Jabez 50 54 116 141 145 146 James 144 Jane 73 Jemima 122 Jeremiah 51 118 120 140 142 Jerusha 121 Jesse 77 122 Joan 114 Joanna 116-118 Joel 115 117 John 56 122 Jonathan 121 122 Joseph 48 52 73 83 91 114-117 144 Kitty 122 Lana 122 Lester 117 Levi 118 Lois 117 121 Lucia 118 Lydia 121 Mary 116 118 121 123 Mehitable 118 Melicent Wills 126 Mercy 116 118 Miner 121 Moses 45 122 Mr 28 Mrs Ephraim 98 Nathaniel 109 118 120 Olive 121 Oliver 118 Orson 117 Pamela 117 Pelatiah 115 121 Percy 117 Phebe

WEST (continued)
 118 Priscilla 121 122
 Prudence 96 116 118 121
 122 Rebecca 118 122 Renda
 117 Roger 122 Ruby 121 122
 Rufus 45 116 117 Ruth 97
 116-118 Salome 117 Samuel
 12 96 114-116 144 Samuel
 Jr 144 Samuel Sr 116 Sarah
 83 114 116-118 Sherman 117
 Solomon 121 122 Solomon Jr
 122 Stephen 115 116 118
 120 121 Submit 116 Susan
 118 Susanna 121 122 Sylvia
 122 Thankful 118 121
 Tryphena 116 William 22 44
 116 117 126 Zadoc 117
 Zebulon 23 96 101 102 104
 109 115 118-121 123 138
 139 142 144 Zerviah 121
WESTON, Sarah 81
WHEELER, Ebenezer 47 Mary
 81 Nathl 47
WHIPPLE, Abraham 45 Noah 50
 Thomas 12
WHITCOMB, Joseph 45 47
WHITE, Ann 32 Sarah 63
WHITEFIELD, Mr 42 111
WHITING, Joseph 30
WHITON, Ammi 133 Anna 133
 Calvin 35 133 134 142
 Elijah 133 Elijah Sr 133
 Erastus 133 Hannah 133
 Luther 133 Marcia 133
 Maria 133 Martha 133
 Matilda 133 Stephen 35 133
 Stephen 2d 134 Sybil 133
 Vodicea 133
WHITTLESEY, Lydia M 68
 Samuel 140 142
WILES, Joshua 12 18 29
WILLES, John 9 Joshua 9
 Joshua Sr 9 Samuel 9
WILLETT, Nathaniel 13
WILLEY, Asa 108 142 Calvin
 104 105 140-142 145 Eliza
 Hall 108 Elizabeth Mary
 108 George Parsons 108
 Harriet Maria 108 James

WILLEY (continued)
 Marshall 108 John Calvin
 108 Letitia N 108 Lucretia
 Green 108 Mary Ann 108 Mr
 106 107 Nabby 108 Sally
 108 Sarah Jane 108 Sidney
 Brainard 108
WILLIAMS, Abigail 36
 Augustus-Davenport 37
 Aurelia 36 Charles-Albert
 37 Damaris 36 David-Burt
 37 Doct 37 38 Dr 42
 Eliakim 37 Eliakim H 36 37
 109 Eliakim Hall 36
 Emeline 37 Isaac 36 37
 John 36 Mary 36-38 Mary-
 Burt 37 Mary-Damaris-
 Aurelia 37 Mortimer-Hall
 37 Nathan 36 37 Rev Doctor
 39 Rev Dr 35 42 Ruth 36
 Samuel 47 Sarah 37 Sophia-
 Maria 37 Stephen 36
 Theodosicus-Dickerman 37
 William 36 37
WILLIS, Jonathan 143
WILLS, Azariah 44 57 71 Col
 61 72 Elizabeth 32 71 95
 Gideon 71 Jemima 71 Joshua
 69-72 138 139 144 Joshua
 Jr 71 Lieut 86 94 Melicent
 71 Miss 113 Mr 72 Nancy 64
 71 Roxalana 63 71 Solo 47
 60 Solomon 32 44-50 52 54-
 57 63 71 79 95 104 139 140
 142 144 Wareham 71
WINSLOW, Maj-Gen 44
WOLCOTT, Charles 9 Henry 5
 9 12 18 20 Maj 44 Roger 8
 9 11 Simon 12 18 Simon Jr
 5
WOOD, Asa 45 56 Charles 56
 Esther 125
WOODWARD, Aaron 52
WORKS, Abigail 89
WRIGHT, Jonathan 45 Samuel
 50
WYLLIS, Hezekiah 30 John P
 56
WYLLYS, Hez 18 Samuel 13

YEOMANS, Abigail 93 Amy 93
  Anna 93 David 93 Elijah 52
  92 93 Elijah Jr 93 Elisha
  92 93 Eunice 93 Hannah 93
  Jerusha 92 93 Joanna 93
  John 28 92 143 John Jr 92
  93 Jonathan 93 Joseph 92
  Mary 92 93 Melicent 71
  Molly 93 Oliver 46 47 58

YEOMANS (continued)
  92 93 Ruth 92 Sarah 93
  Stephen 92 Susanna 92
  Thomas 92
YOUNG, Alfred 8 142
  Benjamin L 141 146
  Eliphalet 140-142 145 Mrs
  B L 98